Cloud Computing 101:
A Primer for Project Managers

by Patrick D. Allen, PMP

Other books by Patrick D. Allen:

Information Operations Planning
(Artech House)

ISBN-13: 978-1508504368
ISBN-10: 1508504369

Printed in the US by CreateSpace
Also available on Kindle

Dedication

To the great minds that created
the Cloud and Hadoop.

Table of Contents

Foreword

It seems that today's world is full of information-technology terms that we use on a daily basis but that only a small percentage of us fully understand. Our lexicon is full of colloquialisms like "big data" and "data mining" and it seems that everyone is aware of that vast storage area in the sky affectionately named "the cloud." But the prevailing opinion, as stated by Cameron Diaz in the movie *The Sex Tape,* is that "Nobody understands the Cloud!"

In this book and through presentations and lectures delivered over the last few years, Patrick Allen has masterfully translated an extremely complex subject into the straightforward language of the Project Manager who must employ this ubiquitous capability to deliver products and services. His simple yet elegant explanations of the architecture, technology and systems that encompass cloud computing, coupled with his "real world" examples of how these capabilities enhance our lives, provide just the right level of knowledge and understanding for managing projects that intersect with or employ these technologies. Most impressive, though, is the way he ties each chapter and topic to the Process Groups and Knowledge areas of the Project Management Body of Knowledge (PMBOK®), the international standard for project management and the Project Manager's primary reference. He takes time throughout the text to provide answers to the key question, "If I am the project manager, what should I be looking for at this point and what questions should I be asking of the project team?"

Dr. Allen is an exceptional writer and lecturer whose passion for the subject is only surpassed by his desire to articulate it in a useful form to his fellow project managers. Whether you use this manuscript as a text for understanding cloud computing or simply as an aid to identifying the intersection of "the cloud" with the delivery of your project, you will find this book to be more of a story than an intellectual exercise. In a pinch, simply referring to the passages that address what the project manager should be looking for/asking questions about if he/she encounters a particular cloud structure, will establish your credibility and identify the maturity level of your project. Dr. Allen has taken a doctorate-level course and boiled it down to the essential elements of information that project managers need to meet their deliverables. A quick read, this book is sure to become a part of the project manager's professional library.

—Michael D. Berendt, PMP, PMI® RMP, ASEP
President, I C Data Inc.

Chapter 1:
Introduction

Purpose

The purpose of this book is to provide project managers (PMs) and non-technical readers with a basic understanding of the three primary types of clouds, cloud security, cloud pricing, cloud computing and the questions they should ask when clouds and their projects intersect.

No Prerequisites

This book was written for the non-technical reader. It does not require the reader to have technical skills or extensive project management experience. You do not need to know how to program or design networks to understand the new mental models of cloud computing.

This book distinguishes between what you need to know about clouds and what you don't need to know in order to understand the basics and be conversant in cloud computing concepts. For example, it is useful to understand why cloud computing has made parallel processing available to the masses, but you don't need to know how to actually write and run map-reduce programs in a cloud. While it is useful to understand some of the basic security issues and best security practices associated with clouds, one does not need to become a cloud security expert. Understanding some of the cost drivers behind Utility Clouds is important for project management, but you don't need to be a costing expert.

All learning involves comparing and contrasting something new to something you already know. This book starts with familiar concepts, then walks the reader through the new concepts of the various types of clouds, and the benefits and limitations of each.

This book is based on the successful Project Management Institute (PMI) Baltimore Chapter seminar series, which has helped those unfamiliar with cloud computing to obtain a functioning understanding of the basics of cloud computing.

Why Clouds Are Important

Cloud computing is here to stay. At some time in the future an even better approach to computation, data processing and storage will be invented, but cloud computing is definitely having a revolutionary effect on many walks of life right now. Commercial, government and academic realms are all achieving specific benefits in a range of projects, such as health care, business processes, managed services, fraud detection, marketing and societal studies. Individuals also benefit from large-scale storage accessible from anywhere, improved entertainment selection and delivery, and greater convenience (though sometimes at the expense of substantially reduced privacy).

Because of the rapidly expanding list of fields in which cloud computing is making inroads, many more projects will be involved in cloud computing in some way. This means that Project Managers will become involved in cloud computing more frequently, whether they want to be or not. It is therefore important for PMs to become familiar with the basic concepts and terminology of cloud computing so that they can effectively operate in the modern world.

Cloud computing is revolutionary, with new concepts that are substantially different from legacy computing and database structures. As a result, these new concepts or mental models must be understood by those who plan to be using cloud computing.

For example, having your IT infrastructure provided by a third party offsite from your offices is significantly different from the traditional "own your own" IT infrastructure. The data structures of Data-focused Clouds and Big Data are substantially different from legacy relational database structures. (Big Data is defined by Gartner as "high volume, high velocity, and/or high variety information assets that require new forms of processing to enable enhanced decision making, insight discovery and process optimization." - Wikipedia, Big Data, 2014) The ability for the masses to be able to perform parallel processing on petabytes worth of data is a definite cultural and technological breakthrough.

This book attempts to convey these new mental models about cloud computing by comparing and contrasting these new features to legacy IT and data processing features. If the computation and data problems your project is trying to solve are relatively small and manageable, legacy hardware and software are likely to be sufficient for your project's purposes. However, if your project is encountering significantly large data feeds, or requires surge IT infrastructure, or the need to coordinate among widely distributed locations, cloud computing offers alternatives not previously available.

As with any new technology, each of the three types of clouds have strengths and limitations. The advantages and disadvantages of the three types of clouds, the three main types of Service Models (IaaS, PaaS, SaaS), and the four types of deployment models (public, community, private and hybrid) all need to be considered by the PM. (All of these terms and models will be described later.) The PM's organization should also weigh the options for using home-built clouds versus third-party clouds.

Hopefully this book will help to dispel some of the mystery and hype associated with cloud computing and give many readers that "Aha!" moment.

Why Clouds Are Important to PMs

Because cloud computing is here to stay, PMs are increasingly likely to encounter situations in which cloud computing will have an impact on their project—whether they want it to or not. As cloud computing becomes more commonly used in commercial, academic, government and military systems, PMs will need to be aware of the strengths and limitation of clouds and their appropriateness or inappropriateness for specific projects.

Often, a PM may not have a choice as to whether to use a cloud in a project, especially if a boss, customer, or sponsor states "You *will* use cloud computing on this project!" If you ask why, you may hear, "Because everyone else is using them!" So while you as the PM may not be able to decide *whether* using a cloud is appropriate for a project, you should at least be able to influence which *type* of cloud to use and how to use it.

When clouds are being discussed, PMs need to make sure everyone understands which type of cloud is being considered. There are currently three basic types of clouds, each with specific capabilities and limitations. Some of these clouds also provide different "service models," which define which types of cloud services are provided to different users. In addition, there are four "deployment models" for clouds.   A deployment model is a way to deploy a cloud or combination of clouds, which will be described later. Each cloud service model and deployment model has its own advantages and disadvantages.

With so many types of clouds, cloud service models, and cloud deployment models, it is critical for a PM to be able to correctly distinguish between each. Otherwise, confusion will result among team members, customers and service providers, which can lead to expectations not being met.   Unmet expectations are bad for business.

If the PM can distinguish between the different types of clouds, service models, deployment models, and their relative strengths and limitations, the PM will be able to:

- Effectively manage the project team and stakeholder expectations
- Effectively plan, execute and monitor projects that involve clouds
- Help your organization and customers avoid costly mistakes
- Guide your organization to effectively leverage new cloud-based capabilities.

To achieve these benefits, the PM will need to:

- Distinguish between different types of clouds
- Be able to describe the capabilities and limitations of each type of cloud
- Be conversant in cloud terminology
- Be able to adequately initiate, plan, execute, monitor and eventually close out a project that uses a cloud

This book is intended to provide PMs with these four skills, as well as to help them understand:

- The basics of clouds and how they work
- How to make clouds work for you and your project
- How to avoid the common pitfalls when using clouds

The book also provides:

- Sets of questions to help ensure that you and your project get what you need out of a cloud
- A mapping of the contents of key chapters to the process groups and knowledge areas in the PMBOK® Guide

This book introduces these concepts to the PM and provides many examples. It also provides an easy reference for PMs not only for definitions, but also for the questions PMs need to ask, and how the various elements of cloud computing map to the PMBOK® Guide. In addition, the appendices are designed for someone who wants to prepare cloud class materials for others, as well as provide a basic knowledge check for the reader.

Contact Information

Feedback to the author is welcome. This is especially true if readers find that something in this book needs updating. This is a fast-moving field, and publishing this book on Kindle and CreateSpace provides the ability to quickly generate updates to help keep the contents of this book current. Contact the author at:

Dr. Patrick D. Allen, PMP
Johns Hopkins University Applied Physics Laboratory
11100 Johns Hopkins Road
Laurel, MD 20723-6099

Patrick.Allen@PatrickAllenPubs.com
http://www.PatrickAllenPubs.com

Chapter 2:
What Is a Cloud?

What Is a Cloud?

We will start with the National Institute of Standards and Technology (NIST) definition, and then present a definition that clarifies key aspects of cloud computing so that a novice can better understand what it is and why it is different.

The NIST definition states:

> Cloud computing is a model for enabling convenient, on-demand network access to a shared pool of configurable computing resources (e.g., networks, servers, storage, applications, and services) that can be rapidly provisioned and released with minimal management effort or service provider interaction. (Mell and Grance, 2011)

While this is a completely accurate description of cloud computing, it is not very useful for a person new to cloud computing. What does a cloud look like? How does it work? Why is it different?

No, Really—What's a Cloud?

For a large-scale cloud as shown in Figure 2.1, a cloud is:

1. A big building somewhere that has lots of electrical power available;
2. Contains a huge number of hard drives (HDs), usually all of the same type;
3. Allows remote access to use that computing power and memory;

4. Often uses virtual machines (VMs) on processors that provide familiar operating systems configurations on demand; and

5. May include an advanced distributed file system to run large-scale parallel programs on huge data sets.

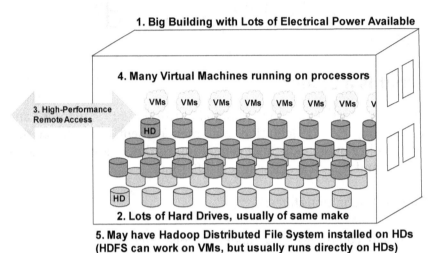

Figure 2.1: A Example of a Large-Scale Cloud

Looking from the outside of a large-scale cloud building, you will see a big building with lots of electric power running into it and a huge cooling system to make sure the equipment inside doesn't overheat. The amount of power consumption is huge! According to a recent report by Mark Mills, "The average square foot of a data center uses 100 to 200 times more electricity than does a square foot of a modern office building." (Mills, 2013) There will also be high-speed Internet connections to the building to handle all of the data flowing into and out of the cloud in the building.

Looking from the inside of a cloud building, one starts with a hard drive on a tray, then a bunch of trays of hard drives stacked within a rack, then lots of racks stacked next to each other in a row, then rows and rows of racks filling the floor, until finally almost every floor of the building is filled with these rows of racks. The size of these large-scale clouds can be truly astounding.

Not physically visible to an observer inside the building are the virtual machines running on processors (like traditional CPUs) in some types of clouds, or advanced distributed file systems on other types of clouds. Which types of clouds have which of these two features will be described in Chapter 3, but all clouds have the hard drives, the electrical power, and some sort of communications connection.

Sizes of Clouds

While these large-scale clouds are becoming more common, a cloud does not have to be large. One of my Applied Physics Laboratory colleagues built his own fourteen-node cloud using commodity hard drives and three inexpensive fans that fit into a 6U custom aluminum holding and cooling frame that could fit on a table. It had sufficient cooling from the fans to be maintained in a room-temperature environment.

Thus, clouds don't have to be large. Small clouds also match the NIST definition. However, the economies of scale provided by cloud computers are greatest when clouds are *big*. As will be seen below, the use of commodity hardware and the automated testing, monitoring and replacement of hardware in a cloud is what makes large cloud clusters cost-effective. The "Principle of Economies of Scale" apply to clouds, so the most cost-effective clouds tend to be huge and operated by third-party cloud service providers (CSPs) such as Amazon Web Services, Google, IBM SmartCloud, Rackspace, Verizon/Terremark and others. Size matters in clouds. Smaller clouds tend to be built and used by individuals or organizations interested in specific types of use, but those individuals or organizations also retain the burden of maintaining these purpose-built clouds.

Benefits and Risks of Clouds

Cloud computing can provide the following benefits:

- **Cloud computing offers lower Information Technology (IT) costs through a "pay only for what you use" model.** The initial purchase and maintenance of computer assets for organizations *can* be substantially reduced through cloud computing. We emphasize the word "can" here because not every organization or business model will actually be able to realize significant economic benefits from the reduced IT infrastructure costs through the use of cloud computing. Even so, enough organizations have been able to realize significant economic benefits, thereby increasing the spread and popularity of cloud computing.

- **Cloud computing offers better visibility in IT costs.** Since companies that use third-party cloud service providers (CSPs) must pay for those services, the costs of IT support become more visible. This also makes it easier to calculate a return on investment in IT support.

- **Cloud computing offers rapid deployment and downsizing of IT resources.** Since users only pay for what they use, there will be times when users want to significantly increase or decrease the IT resources they are using. Cloud computing offers rapid expansion of available IT resources, allowing for quick and flexible scalability to user IT resources. This feature is particularly useful for organizations that have major surge activities, such as census data, or start-up organizations seeking to minimize initial IT investment.

- **Cloud computing offers built-in data redundancy and therefore resilience.** Most CSPs use common hardware across their clouds. This allows CSPs to be able to reliably monitor and predict when hard drives are going bad, and transfer the data prior to a crash. In addition, automated data replication in the cloud helps preclude a single point of failure via automated data redundancy.

- **Cloud computing *allows* for solutions to a wide range of large data problems that were not previously economical to solve.** We emphasize the word "allows" because not every Big Data problem is readily solved by cloud computing. However, Big Data analysis using cloud computing has found many previously undetected relationships among data elements. This has resulted in either economic benefits, increased understanding, or both. For example, cloud computing helped determine the relationship between the weather and the types of products customers purchase from bakeries. This reduced bakeries' daily costs due to wastage or due to the opportunity costs of running out of product. The relationship between the weather and food-type sales was not previously known until cloud computing and Big Data analysis was performed. (IBM 2011)

- **Cloud computing can facilitate finding useful information in unstructured data.** Structured data is like the data you have in a spreadsheet—data elements organized by rows and columns. These databases structured by rows and columns are called relational databases. Cloud computing can also work on finding relationships among unstructured data, such as web pages, text files, and binary files. This increases the scope of data analysis and business intelligence organizations can perform on their existing and emerging data sets.

This is not an exhaustive list of benefits, and other benefits will be described later in the book.

While cloud computing has a number of increased benefits, it also carries some *increased risks*, especially in the realm of security. For example, when cloud computing services were first being provided by third-party vendors, this brought about specific types of new security issues that were not a problem with traditional on-premises computers. Most of these new problems have either been solved or are in the process of being solved, but all of these new security and availability concerns need to be carefully addressed when considering the risks of cloud computing with respect to your project.

Another key difference with cloud computing is that if one is using third-party CSPs, the data does not physically reside on your organization's premises. This can create significant anxiety and genuine concerns, especially in terms of data availability.

Cloud Adoption Trends

The rate at which cloud adoption has been trending over time reflects the preceding list of benefits and risks associated with cloud computing. The greater the interest in cost savings and increased data processing and storage capabilities, the more likely the organization will adopt a cloud. The greater the concern about security or not having physical control of their data, the less interest there will be in moving to the cloud.

In September 2012, Tech Target surveyed a range of organizations to determine their cloud adoption rates and probable future cloud adoption. What they found was that both public and private clouds had reached about 25% penetration within IT, while hybrid cloud adoption lagged at 16%. (Note that a Cloud Adoption Index of 100% would mean that everyone is using a cloud.)

In March 2013, Tech Target repeated the survey and found that the rate of cloud adoption had not increased significantly. Some of the reasons cited by organizations for not adopting clouds cited lack of control over the cloud environment as the main reason for non-adoption. One third (33%) felt that their data centers were not sufficiently virtualized to make the transition to the cloud smooth or efficient. Security was still a significant concern; 31% of the respondents cited this as their reason to forego cloud computing at that time. (Boisvert, 2013)

However, a September 2014 article from Evolve IP surveyed IT professionals and executives on cloud adoption. According to their follow-up survey of 1,257 executives and IT professionals, 90% agreed that the future model of IT is definitely cloud computing, and 81% of all respondents had already deployed at least one service in the cloud. (Mennig, 2014)

So while there are still valid concerns about cloud computing, especially in the areas of security and control over the data, it appears that cloud computing continues to gain in popularity and its adoption.

Chapter 3:
The Three Types of Clouds

There are three basic types of cloud:

Type 1 Cloud: Storage Cloud: For example, the type used for home user online back-ups

Type 2 Cloud: Utility Cloud: The Type 2 Cloud has three basic "service models":

- Infrastructure as a Service (IaaS): Making an IT Infrastructure available to users

- Platforms as a Service (PaaS): Making a development platform available to users

- Software as a Service (SaaS): Making some software commonly available to users

Type 3 Cloud: Data-focused Cloud: Allows parallel, distributed processing via map-reduce programs, and usually uses Hadoop Distributed File System (HDFS)

Each of these three types of clouds and the three basic service models of the Type 2 Cloud will be described in more detail later.

Note that while this book refers to Cloud Types 1, 2, and 3, the rest of the world does not yet do so. The reason we do so in this book is that we have found through the repeated classes presented on the topic, that defining the three types of clouds in this way makes them easier to remember and distinguish. The combination of these three types and the picture below (see Figure 3.1) has been a very effective memory device for those who wish to differentiate between these three types of clouds.

Figure 3.1 shows that the Type 1 Cloud, the Storage Cloud, just has lots and lots of memory. That's it. You can't do computations on a Type 1 Cloud, and you can't do parallel processing or Big Data calculations. All you can do is put data into it and retrieve it at a later date. Storage Clouds are used to store and retrieve data, such as providing online back-ups of photographs, music, and electronic documents.

Cloud Type 1: Storage Cloud	Lots of Memory		
Cloud Type 2: Utility Cloud	Lots of Memory +	Virtual Machines	
Cloud Type 3: A Data-focused Cloud	Lots of Memory +	Hadoop Distributed + File System	Hadoop map-reduce

Figure 3.1: The Three Types of Clouds

The Type 2 Cloud has lots of memory, plus a wide range of virtual machines. We will describe virtual machines later, but for now simply consider virtual machines as electronic (non-physical) personal computers that can be created when needed and deleted when no longer needed. The Type 2 Cloud provides a lot of computing power, and can be used to replicate much of the infrastructure of an organization's current Information Technology infrastructure. Type 2 Clouds can also provide specialized development platforms and software, but they are not designed to perform the parallel processing of Big Data analysis. Type 2 Clouds can also provide storage like a Type 1 Cloud, but cloud service providers that provide both differentiate which portion of the cloud will be used for storage versus used for utility.

Type 3 Clouds are Data-focused Clouds. They are designed to run large-scale parallel processing programs called "map-reduce" programs in order to do Big Data analysis. Data-focused Clouds can't be used to provide the generic Type 2 or Utility Cloud, and so are not applicable to run, for example, your legacy office software. Data-focused Clouds can also perform the function of a Storage Cloud, and also differentiate which parts of the cloud are used for each.

Early on in cloud computing, the Type 3 Cloud had the Hadoop Distributed File System installed on virtual machines (VMs).

However, it was soon found to be much faster to install the Hadoop Distributed File System directly on a hard drive with an operating system, so the VMs are not usually used in a Type 3 Cloud. (One exception appears to be OpenStack's Sahara Project.) (Sahara, 2014)

Note that HDFS is a file system just as NFS is the traditional Network File System found in legacy office networks. NFS is usually used as the network storage and retrieval system on a Storage Cloud or on a Utility Cloud. Some Storage Clouds use HDFS instead of NFS to provide automatic triple redundancy, as will be described later. Utility Clouds run NFS since the legacy applications used in a Utility Cloud run on NFS. If a single CSP provides the services of all three types of clouds (Storage, Utility, and Data-focused), their cloud architecture is divided into parts using NFS and parts using HDFS.

This book uses the term "Data-focused Cloud" rather than just "Data Cloud," which is often the term used for the Type 3 Cloud. The reason for this choice is that just calling a Type 3 Cloud a "Data Cloud" is confusing to those new to cloud computing. Data exists in Storage Clouds and Utility Clouds, so why is a Data Cloud different? The answer is that in a Data-focused Cloud, the architecture of the Type 3 Cloud is focused on the large-scale manipulation and analysis of the data, rather than just data storage or traditional use of data in an office setting.

Modifying Figure 2.1, Figure 3.2 shows how these three types of clouds appear within the concept of a large-scale cloud. The first three elements (1 - big building with lots of electrical power; 2 - lots of hard drives usually of the same make; and 3 - high performance remote access communications) are shared by all three types of clouds. Furthermore, those three elements define all of the components of a Storage Cloud—the Type 1 Cloud.

To get to a Type 2 Cloud, one needs to add item 4 (lots of virtual machines running on processors in order to provide the necessary compute power). To get to a Type 3 Cloud, one needs to (usually) not include the VMs (item 4), but to include item 5, the Hadoop Distributed File System.

For all three types of clouds, users can either build and maintain their own clouds, or contract with a third-party cloud service provider (CSP) to provide access to one or more types of clouds. Chapter 8 describes sample cloud service level agreements (SLAs) available from various CSPs.

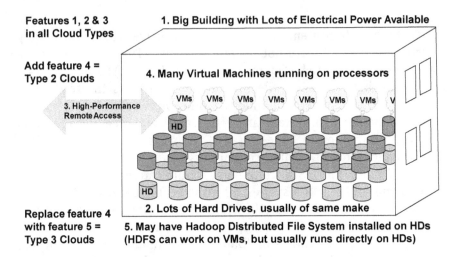

Figure 3.2: How the Three Types of Clouds Differ

Figures 3.1 and 3.2 should help the reader remember the three basic types of clouds and how they differ from each other. Appendix A provides a "knowledge check" to help understand how well you remember the three types of clouds and their distinctions, as well how well you can explain why it is important to be able to distinguish between these different types of clouds.

Chapter 4:
Type 1 Cloud:
Storage Cloud

How Storage Clouds Work

Type 1 Clouds consist of huge amounts of memory accessible by authorized remote users. As described in the previous chapter, large-scale storage clouds are usually large buildings with lots of electrical power, huge numbers of commodity hard drives for memory, and high-speed access to the cloud.

How does the Storage Cloud provide protection against data loss? Most storage clouds automatically generate back-ups of whatever is stored in them. Since the Storage Cloud service provider (CSP) is using commodity hard drives to store all this data, there is a chance that any hard drive might crash and lose the data that was stored on it. To prevent this, the CSP automatically makes a copy of the data on a second hard drive, and usually makes a copy on a third hard drive on a physically different rack.

The result of this triple redundancy is that the chance of anyone's data being lost when stored in a Type 1 Cloud is very, very low. Since this is much better redundancy than is available in most homes or even offices, there is a greater assurance that the data stored in a Storage Cloud won't be lost by accident. The bigger the cloud of available storage, the greater the chance that the data you store in a Storage Cloud will still exist even if one, or even two, hard drives crash in a short period of time.

A few examples of the many companies that provide cloud storage services include:

- Comcast's online back-up service

- eBay's online back-up service
- Amazon's Simple Storage System (S3)

Benefits of Storage Clouds

Users can place their photographs, music, videos, documents, electronic books, scanned papers, and any other data into the Storage Cloud with the intent of retrieving it later. This not only allows for protection against loss of data when a home computer crashes or is lost in a house fire, it allows users to access these remotely stored items from wherever they can access the Internet. User access to data stored in a Type 1 Cloud can occur from home, school, a friend's house, while on travel, from Mars (well, not yet Mars), or wherever the user has Internet access.

Companies and other organizations can also benefit from cloud storage. Rather than having to retain hard copies of records in a warehouse or storage shed, a company can have the documents scanned and store them in a Type 1 Cloud. This will reduce storage costs, and increase the chance of the survival of the information in case of disaster. For example, a company could include a Storage Cloud as part of their disaster recovery plan, since the data could be accessed by authorized personnel from a new location after a fire, flood, tornado or earthquake.

If you are a PM on a project that has critical information that needs to be retained, or if you are running a distributed project where geographically remote personnel need to share information, a Storage Cloud can be useful as well. As long as access is properly controlled, this approach to sharing information can be very useful to a project manager.

The CSPs also benefit from the use of redundancy within a Storage Cloud. For example, let's say that 10,000 users are all storing the same popular song. The specific recording of that song will have a unique electronic signature (called a hash) that uniquely identifies it from all other songs or data files. Rather than storing 10,000 copies of this song (or 30,000 copies when including triple redundancy), the cloud storage provider need only store a dozen or so copies of the song. As long as all of the users who stored that song in the Storage Cloud can retrieve that song on demand, it doesn't matter whether it is one of a dozen or one of 10,000. Therefore, the economies of scale increase for a CSP as long as what is being stored by one person is identical to what is being stored by another person.

Note that while using the hash to retain fewer redundant copies of the same file works well for songs, there is little overlap between things like individual photographs. One person's "happy snap" is unlikely to be identical to (or have the same hash as) another person's photograph. So unless the same photo is being stored by many people, there is unlikely to be any comparable economies of scale for the CSP. However, since their cost model is based on storing every user's items uniquely, the CSPs will still make a profit.

Limitations and Issues of Storage Clouds

While a Storage Cloud is excellent for data storage and retrieval, that's all it does. One cannot place data into a Storage Cloud and then run programs or applications on that data while it is still in a cloud. No computational services, such as word processing or spreadsheet software, are available on a storage cloud. There are no opportunities to perform Big Data analysis within a Storage Cloud. A Type 1 Cloud is simply designed to perform receipt, redundant storage, and on-demand retrieval of what is stored within it.

So if you are a project manager and your boss wants you to run Big Data analysis on the company's archives within the Storage Cloud, you can (kindly) inform your boss that such a function is not available in that type of cloud. The company's archives would first have to be transferred to a Type 3 Data-focused Cloud in order to perform that analysis.

Security of the data stored in the cloud is an issue for all three types of clouds. This issue is addressed more thoroughly in Chapter 7. For now, we simply state that if the data you plan to store in a Storage Cloud is sensitive (such as personally identifiable information or PII), then you probably want to take the following steps:

1. Ensure an access control mechanism with strong authentication is in place so that only the personnel you want access to the data are on the access list

2. Ensure that the data being sent to storage or retrieved is adequately encrypted in transit so no one can read it coming or going

3. Ensure that the data is adequately encrypted while being stored.

(Adequate encryption means that the size of the encryption key is sufficiently large, the encryption algorithms strong and well-defined, and that the underlying key management system is not easily compromised. A project's or organization's supporting security personnel should be familiar with, and be able to provide, these encryption features.)

Regarding encryption "at rest" (that is, while it is in storage), it makes sense to encrypt PII or company proprietary information. Other information that is publically available, such as company flyers, logos, or maps to facilities, do not need to be encrypted (unless it is a master copy that needs to be retained and unchangeable).

Another issue to consider is what happens when there is a power outage in the Storage Cloud's region and not where the users are located. In the past, if a company had a power outage and no generator backup was available, the company just made do until power was back up. Now, with the company's data potentially stored at a geographically remote location at the CSP, what does the company do when it has power and is ready to do business, but the access to its stored files is not available? There is no easy answer to this problem, which we will discuss further in Chapter 8 on arranging to use a cloud and service level agreements (SLAs).

Storage Clouds and the PMBOK® Guide

The PMBOK® Guide describes the process groups and the knowledge areas performed by the project manager. This section will discuss where Type 1 Clouds might be involved in the five process groups and the ten knowledge areas of project management. Note that if the PM's organization already regularly uses a Storage Cloud, the organization will probably already have standard operating procedures (SOPs) covering many of these topics.

Process Groups:

Initiating Process Group:

During project initiation, the PM needs to determine whether a Storage Cloud will be used to support the project. The use of a

Storage Cloud may be mandated by the organization, or the use may be selected by the PM. Whatever the cause, a succinct description of why a Storage Cloud will be used and how it will be used is essential. The PM should also ensure that if a Type 1 Cloud is selected to support a project, that it is the most appropriate of the three types of clouds to support that project.

Planning Process Group:

If a Storage Cloud has been selected for use in this project, then a storage CSP will need to be selected during planning (assuming the organization does not already have a standing agreement with a storage CSP). If the use of a Storage Cloud to support a project is an innovation, then how the Storage Cloud will be used to support the existing or new business model will need to be described. If the use of a Storage Cloud is common at the PM's organization, then simply refer to or modify the existing SOP.

For example, if the Storage Cloud will be used as a source of data as part of a disaster recovery program, then how the data will be accessed by whom and from where should all be included in the project plan.

Further planning will be required for determining whether and how which types of the data will be encrypted in transit and/or at rest on the storage cloud. Creating the access control list for who from each location has access to which data will also be important.

Risk planning will include assessing the risk of a data breach, and what to do if the data is temporarily unavailable from the CSP (such as due to a power failure at the CSP site).

Executing Process Group:

During project execution, the PM or his designee will need to set up the access control and determine who on the team has which access to the Storage Cloud and why. The purpose behind the use of the Storage Cloud will determine who gets access, can send data to storage, and retrieve or delete data from storage.

Monitoring and Controlling Process Group:

The PM needs to monitor (or have someone monitor) the access control list to the data stored in the cloud to ensure it is current. For example, if someone leaves the company, you may have retrieved the key to the building and removed the former employee's access to the local network, but don't forget to remove that person's access to what is stored in the cloud. Other features to monitor are whether the use of the cloud for storage are meeting the expected benefits, or whether there are problems with the efficiency of the system. Making sure the CSP meets the criteria for availability as described in the service level agreement will also be important. It is also good business practice to have your organization's penetration testers periodically check that the data being transmitted and at rest are actually encrypted.

Closing Process Group:

If the use of the Storage Cloud will continue beyond the end of the project, then the PM needs to ensure the access control is correctly closed out. If the Storage Cloud will no longer be used at the end of the project, then the final disposition of the data in the Storage Cloud will need to be addressed.

Knowledge Areas:

Stakeholder Management Knowledge Area:

The PM will need to determine which team members and other stakeholders will need access to the data stored in the cloud. How often and how quickly they will need to access the data will define the requirements for responsiveness and availability. Business needs and constraints on who can access sensitive information will determine which stakeholders get access to which data.

Communications Knowledge Area:

Communications to stakeholders should include how the Storage Cloud will be used to support the project. In addition, the PM needs to communicate the plan for how secure communications of data to and from the cloud will be ensured and monitored during the project. Communications with the CSP management will also be essential, such as when issues occur that need to be resolved.

Risk Knowledge Area:

Before selecting a Storage Cloud, list and evaluate the risks of using a Storage Cloud. Identify the risks, perform risk analysis, and plan risk responses. After selecting a Storage Cloud, monitor the communications and data stored in the cloud for any changes in the risk factors.

Procurement Knowledge Area:

Procurement of a Storage Cloud service level agreement (SLA) is a prerequisite to using a Storage Cloud. If the PM's organization already has a standing arrangement with a Storage Cloud CSP, this step is straightforward.

Cost Knowledge Area:

The use of a Storage Cloud will entail a cost that must be planned and managed. While storing data in a Storage Cloud is relatively inexpensive compared to physically storing hard copies of data, there are monthly costs that need to be estimated, budgeted, and monitored throughout the project life cycle.

Integration Knowledge Area:

The use of a Storage Cloud must be integrated into the organization's business model. How will it be used? What will it be used for? Who will have access to the data and why? How long will the data be stored before being aged off? If the Storage Cloud will be used as part of a continuity of operations plan, how will it be used and how will you train for it?

Scope Knowledge Area:

How will the Storage Cloud be used within your business model? How much data will be stored in the Storage Cloud each month? If the scope of use changes over time, how will that scope creep be managed?

Time Knowledge Area:

When will operations be transitioned to start using a Storage Cloud? Or for a particular project, when will the project start using the Storage Cloud as part of its operations? Is the cloud service provider on-board with the transition time, magnitude of data stored and retrieved each month?

Quality Knowledge Area:

What is the data retrieval time, and does this match the service level agreement (SLA)? How is the quality of service measured according to the SLA? Who will monitor the performance of the Storage Cloud provider and how?

Human Resources Knowledge Area:

If the Storage Cloud is storing personally identifiable information (PII), then the access control for PII stored in the cloud needs to be properly instituted and managed.

Chapter 5:
Type 2 Cloud: Utility Cloud

Overview

This chapter begins with a description of virtual machines (VMs). If the reader is familiar with VMs *and* how they are used in clouds, feel free to skip this introduction.

The second part of this chapter describes the Utility Cloud, which we are calling a Type 2 Cloud. We describe how these types of clouds work in general, and the advantages and disadvantages of Type 2 Clouds.

The third part describes the three primary variants or "service models" of Type 2 Clouds (Infrastructure as a Service [IaaS], Platform as a Service [PaaS], and Software as a Service [SaaS]). This section also covers a number of niche variants under these three main subcomponents, whereby cloud service providers attempt to distinguish their offerings from other CSPs.

The fourth part of this chapter discusses the strengths, limitations and benefits of the Type 2 Cloud in general, and specifically for each service model of Type 2 Cloud.

The fifth part presents some of the questions Project Managers should ask of Type 2 Cloud Service Providers.

The last part describes how the Type 2 Cloud might be used by PMs as described by the project management process groups and knowledge areas as described in the PMBOK® Guide.

What Are Virtual Machines?

Virtual machines (VMs) are used extensively in Type 2 Clouds. Therefore, a basic understanding of VMs is important to understanding how Type 2 Clouds work.

There are many definitions for virtual machines:

- "The simulated machine" (Goldberg, 2002)

- "A software implementation of a machine (i.e., a computer) that executes instructions (not programs) like a physical machine" (Wikipedia, Virtual Machine)

- "A virtual machine is a piece of software which allows operating systems to be run 'inside' other operating systems" (Ubuntu, Virtual Machine)

- "A computer within a computer, implemented in software. A virtual machine emulates a complete hardware system, from processor to network card, in a self-contained, isolated software environment, enabling the simultaneous operation of otherwise incompatible operating systems" (Interglot, Virtual Machine)

- "Software that allows you to take a single physical device (e.g., one PC) and run multiple instances of operating systems on it" (Holtsnider and Jaffe, 2006)

For the purposes of this book, we will define a virtual machine as "a software and operating system 'package' that replicates all of the functionality of a personal computer but can run on almost any type of underlying hardware (Linux, Windows, or Unix)."

One key feature of VMs used in Type 2 Clouds is that many VMs can run on a single processor. This provides for multiple VMs of the same type, or even different types and different operating systems, to run on the same CPU. Cloud service providers can run multiple VMs for the same user on the same processor, or even VMs owned by different users on the same processor. (The latter case can also create potential security issues, as will be described in Chapter 7.)

Another feature of VMs is that VMs can be quickly created and deleted on demand. Thousands of VMs are created and deleted every day in most large-scale CSPs. This allows for extremely efficient use of the underlying systems by allowing many opportunities for the processors to not sit idle. Each processor is capable of running multiple VMs of different types at once, and are able to add new VMs and delete old ones on demand.

One key security advantage of VMs is that any number of instances (copies) of a VM can be created from a single master copy. That means that only the master copy of the VM needs to be maintained fully patched and secure; thereafter every instance made from the master copy will also be fully patched. This is much simpler than keeping physical computers fully patched and secure. If physical PCs were being used instead of VMs, the CSP would have to update each PC separately. VMs allow the creation and maintenance of one master copy of each type of VM, significantly reducing the patch and security update process of traditional networks.

A final advantage of VMs is that upon deletion, any malware that happened to infect the VM while it was active is destroyed upon the deletion of the VM (assuming the malware did not embed itself somewhere permanently in the hardware). When a new VM is created from the master copy, any malware that had infected the destroyed copy will not be present on the master copy, nor on any new copies generated from that master copy.

Why Are Virtual Machines Used in Type 2 Clouds?

Cloud service provider (CSP) profits are the result of efficiencies based on scale. The more efficiently a CSP operates, the greater its profits. One way to be extremely efficient is to use only identical hardware. Two key types of hardware are used in Type 2 Clouds: hard drives and processors. We will discuss hard drives first.

Identical hard drives make testing, installing, monitoring and replacing the hardware components very efficient through the use of extensive automation. For example, all of the hard drives should be thoroughly tested so that hard drives with defects can be detected prior to installation in the cloud. The more automated the testing and installation process, the more efficient the process, and therefore the more profitable for the CSP.

Automated monitoring of the hard drives also gives indications and warnings that a hard drive is about to fail, allowing the data on that hard drive to be transferred prior to the actual failure. As described in Chapter 4, multiple copies of data are stored in a cloud for data protection via redundancy. (This is true for all three types of clouds, though different methods to provide redundancy of data are sometimes used in different clouds.) Therefore, CSPs benefit from using identical hardware to maximize scalability and efficiency.

With respect to the processors, using all identical hardware means that different types of users also all have to use the same type of processor. If one user prefers Linux and another prefers Windows as their operating system, how will a CSP provide such variation when all of the hardware is identical?

The answer is for the CSP to provide a wide range of virtual machines that all run on the same type of processor. Different VMs are created for different user needs. For example, at one time, Amazon Web Services provided a menu of over 400 different types of VMs for users to select from, including different combinations of Linux, Windows and Unix operating systems, various releases (such as Windows XP or Window 7), and various service packs (patch levels). AWS has since streamlined their offerings, but still supports many legacy configurations (Amazon EC2 Instances). Most large-scale CSPs that provide Type 2 Clouds provide a wide range of VMs which users can select from to best match their needs.

For example, if you are a business person who uses Windows 7 Service Pack 1 in your office, you would probably want the CSP's Utility Cloud machines to run the version you are using, so that all of your current applications will run without having to upgrade or change your software.

As a result, VMs provide variety and flexibility to the users while the common processors provide scalability and efficiency to the CSP. Moreover, the benefits of VMs in terms of rapid creation and deletion, single master copy, and multiple instances of each VM type also contribute to the scalability and efficiency of the Type 2 Cloud. The use of the master copy ensures that each time a new VM is created, it has the most recent patches and security features. This is a significant improvement in maintenance and security compared to the previous need to individually upgrade each physical machine.

This flexible, on-demand business model allows CSPs to maximize the use of their underlying hardware. By providing the options desired by a given user, each user can obtain the type of computer power desired. Since different users will have peak usage at different times of the day, each processor may be used by multiple users using different types of VMs throughout the course of a day.

Figures 5.1 and 5.2 show a hypothetical use of a cloud with VMs running on some of the 66 available processors in two different time periods respectively. (In this simplistic example, assume only one VM is operating on one processor at a time. In reality, many VMs can run on a single processor. Moreover, clouds have many thousands of processors and not just the 66 in this example.) Company A needs two different VM configurations, Company B needs a third configuration, while Company C needs a fourth VM configuration. In the first time period (Figure 5.1), it so happens that Company A

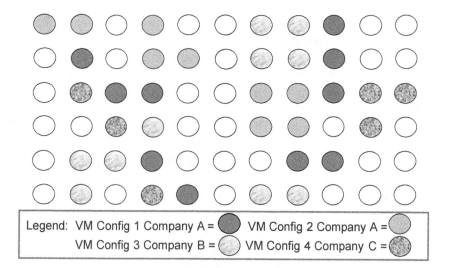

Figure 5.1: Three Companies Using 4 VM Configurations in First Time Period

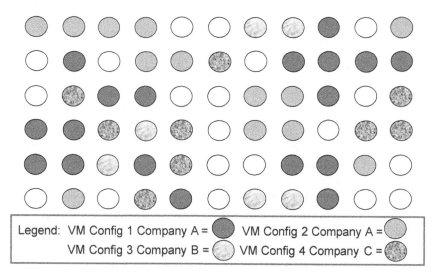

Figure 5.2: Three Companies Using 4 VM Configurations in Second Time Period

requires 10 VMs of configuration 1 and 9 VMs of configuration 2, but in the second time period (Figure 5.2) Company A requires 18 VMs of configuration 1 and 13 VMs of configuration 2. Meanwhile, in the first time period, Company B requires 10 VMs of Configuration 3, but only needs 6 VMs of that same configuration in the second time period. Similarly, Company C requires only 6 VMs of configuration 4 in the first time period, but requires 9 VMs of the same configuration in the second time period.

Note when comparing Figures 5.1 and 5.2, that some of the processors are used by the same company in both time periods, while in the second time period a different company is using the same processor with a different VM, or may be using a processor in the second time period that was unused in the first time period.

The flexibility provided by allowing users to use different types of VMs on identical hardware over time makes Type 2 Clouds very efficient. Chapter 7 will also describe some security concerns that need to be addressed by having different users use the same underlying processors, hypervisor or hardware at the same or different times, as well as some of the solutions CSPs provide to overcome those security concerns.

In addition, multiple VMs of the same or different types can run simultaneously on a single processor. Multiple processors on a motherboard are controlled by a single hypervisor. A hypervisor is software that runs between the VMs and the hardware that facilitates the management of VMs and improves the overall security of the cloud. This further increases the economies of scale by allowing multiple VMs for each processor (rather than one VM per processor), and can leverage the latest technologies for sharing CPU processing cycles of the underlying hardware.

Utility Clouds

This section discusses Type 2 Clouds and what they do and do not provide. We also contrast what Type 2 Clouds offer compared to Type 1 or Type 3 Clouds.

Type 2 Clouds (Utility Clouds) provide an on-demand set of computing resources selected by the user for specified periods of time. The term "on-demand" means that the user can request more or fewer resources over time, and only pay for the number of resources used. Add two more VMs, and the user only pays for two additional VMs. For example, a CSP may charge pennies per gigabyte of memory used per month. (Note that due to strong competition in the CSP community, many CSPs have cost structures so complicated as to require the use of online calculators to determine the price you would pay for a given configuration. See Chapter 8 for details.)

The computing resources made available to users can be "empty" VMs running on commodity hardware (Infrastructure as a Service, described further below), or a development environment (Platform as a Service), or a specific software package (Software as a Service). In addition, there are variants to these computing resources, such as a Desktop as a Service, which provides not only the VM, but also a suite of software that runs on remote desktops.

From the user perspective, a Type 2 Cloud provides the ability to re-create all or part of their current office environment within a Type 2 Cloud, including the same operating system and service pack. This has the advantage of being able to access the company's resources from different locations, and can be used as part of a Continuity of Operations Plan (COOP). Moreover, all of the hardware and many of the operating system maintenance issues are the responsibility of the Cloud Service Provider (CSP) rather than the user. For example, if a disk crashes, the CSP replaces the dying or dead hard drive without the user even being aware of the crash. Operating system patches are performed by the CSP, and rolled into their offering of VMs to customers. Moreover, physical security of the cloud is provided by the CSP, and CSPs often have better physical security than do most companies' data centers.

Many CSPs also provide virtual private clouds (VPCs). VPCs are "reserved" hard drives and processors that can be used only by the paying customer. This precludes the possibility of a hacker using a co-residency attack to get at another user's data, as only one organization's users are allowed on the server. The limited number of users means that some hard drives and processors are likely to be idle, which results in less profit for the CSP than a hardware suite with multiple customers over time. Hence, because they are less efficient, VPCs cost more than general cloud access.

What Type 2 Clouds Do Not Provide

While a Type 2 Cloud provides all of these benefits, there are a number of things the CSP does not provide. Project managers need to be aware of those things that Type 2 Clouds do not provide in order to plan and execute the project and manage expectations.

First, the CSP does not provide any password reset capability. In order to make sure your data is secure on the cloud, the CSP does *not* have access to your password. If you forget your password, you might as well start all over, because the CSP doesn't know your password and can't reset it under any circumstances.

Second, it is essential to encrypt the data you are sending to or retrieving from the cloud. The communications links are often not secure, and you don't want your proprietary or other sensitive data transiting in the clear. So while your communications in your office building might be secure, once it leaves your building, you need to ensure that it is encrypted.

Third, besides encrypting your communications with the cloud, it is a very good idea to encrypt your data when it is at rest in the cloud. This is especially true when not running in a VPC, but it is good practice to encrypt your data at rest in the cloud even in a VPC.

Encryption should start at the local servers and continue across the [communications channel] for data in-flight and data at rest in remote cloud. Both a cloud provider [CSP] and user can supply encryption, so it's important to understand what the public cloud provider [CSP] supplies and the gaps you'll need to fill for top-notch security. (Bigelow, 2014)

Using only CSP encryption is convenient, but that means the provider also has the keys to your sensitive data. Therefore, the user may want to provide all of the encryption capabilities for the data to ensure that the CSP can't see your data. (See additional information about security issues and solutions in the cloud in Chapter 7.)

Fourth, the service level agreement (SLA) the PM negotiates with the CSP limits the liability of the CSP to data lost due to the loss of hardware and insufficient data back-up procedures, and possibly due to a lack of physical security. Power outages at the CSP location that do not affect your organization usually result in only a credit to your organization for temporary loss of availability—not any monetary damages against the CSP. (See Chapter 8 for a discussion of cloud SLAs.)

Fifth, the Type 2 Cloud does not offer parallel processing like a Type 3 (Data-focused) Cloud. If you want to do "Big Data" analysis, you want a Type 3 Cloud, not a Type 2 Cloud. Note, however, that a Type 2 Cloud may be configured as a Database as a Service (DBaaS) cloud, which would allow traditional relational database services and analysis, but would not offer the large-scale Big Data parallel processing services. In addition, the Type 2 Cloud may also provide cloud-based data storage like a Type 1 Cloud.

Type 2 Cloud Service Models and Their Strengths and Limitations

There are three primary "service models" of Type 2 Clouds:

- Infrastructure as a Service (IaaS)
- Platform as a Service (PaaS), and
- Software as a Service (SaaS)

These three service models are listed in order of greatest to least flexibility. Users can run a wide range of VMs and their own software on the VMs in IaaS, but can only run one type of software (or software suite) within SaaS. Conversely, IaaS has the least economy of scale, while SaaS has the most, due to the specialization of the SaaS offering. See Figure 5.3 for how IaaS, PaaS, and SaaS differ within the Type 2 Cloud.

A number of niche variants under these three main service models have also emerged as cloud service providers attempt to distinguish their offerings from other CSPs. These will be described below in the sub-section titled "Other 'X'aaS variants."

Infrastructure as a Service (IaaS) Cloud

An IaaS cloud service model provides the most flexibility of the Type 2 Cloud service models because it provides the basic IT resources: VMs running on common hardware. IaaS allows users to have remote access to the computing power resources they desire, and only pay for those resources when they are used.

On an IaaS, users may select the type or types of VMs they want to run, and then load those VMs with whatever software they have. The user can then place any data and software the user owns onto those VMs and run them as though they were an extension (or replacement of) their legacy office resources. For example, one organization may want to replicate their existing accounts receivable in an IaaS, so they would place their data and application

Cloud Type 1: Storage Cloud		Lots of Memory			

	IaaS	Lots of Memory	+	Virtual Machines	
Cloud Type 2: Utility Cloud	PaaS	Lots of Memory	+	Virtual Machines	& Specific Development Apps & Services
	SaaS	Lots of Memory	+	Virtual Machines	& Specific Software Application

Cloud Type 3: A Data-focused Cloud	Lots of Memory	+	Hadoop Distributed File System	+	Hadoop map-reduce

Figure 5.3: Three Service Models for Type 2 Clouds

software onto those VMs. The largest IaaS provider at the time of this writing is Amazon Web Services.

One of the main benefits of IaaS is that users only pay for what they use when they use it, and additional resources can be obtained almost instantly for only the marginal cost of the additional VMs. This is particularly useful for organizations with periodic surges, such as the US Census Bureau.

New venture start-ups can also benefit by not needing to acquire and install a large IT infrastructure, thereby reducing initial investment costs before positive cash flow kicks in.

Lastly, IaaS is also useful for a distributed organization that needs to share data as well as computing power.

Some concerns about IaaS are the security concerns and availability limitations when the data and computing is performed at a location remote from your organization. These concerns are described in more detail in Chapters 7 and 8 respectively.

Platform as a Service (PaaS) Cloud

PaaS starts out like an IaaS (where VMs are running on commodity hardware), but the CSP adds operating systems, developer tools and applications, and/or web services. (See Figure 5.3 again.) One example of a PaaS is the Google App Engine Development Environment. Note that when the CSP provides the development environment, the user is restricted to using those applications, development tools and services. In a PaaS, the user is not bringing their own office applications and running them in the PaaS. However, the user may be bringing their own code to run and test within the PaaS.

As mentioned above, PaaS has less flexibility than IaaS, but PaaS has more economy of scale, supporting more users at less overall investment. This is due to the financial benefit of specialization by offering a particular type of service rather than a wider range of services.

The greatest benefit from PaaS is that users do not need to pay for their own development environment. Powerful development environments are expensive, so making a development environment available to more users via a PaaS allows more users to develop applications and other software more quickly than without a PaaS. This makes PaaS very useful for Open Source development, as well as for crowd-sourcing projects where some special resources are made available to participants. In general, PaaS is very useful in bringing distributed participants to work in a common environment within the bounds specified by that environment.

The benefits of PaaS also indicate its limitations. Working remotely carries its own security concerns, and working remotely with others increases security concerns. In addition, the capabilities provided by a PaaS development environment are limited to the provider's development tools. Even so, if you are a developer of certain types of software or collaborating on a crowd-sourcing project, a PaaS is an inexpensive way to participate in that environment.

Software as a Service (SaaS) Cloud

SaaS also starts out like an IaaS (running VMs on commodity hardware), but the CSP provides a specific software application or software suite. An example of such a software application is Salesforce, which was originally designed to allow companies to manage and collaborate among geographically distributed sales teams. Salesforce has since added many more features, and provides a suite of software that can be remotely accessed in their clouds (Salesforce Products Overview).

The benefits of SaaS are that users don't need to install software at every location. The SaaS software is accessible anywhere via the web. As long as the user has authorized access, the software can be accessed from any location with an Internet connection. This allows widely distributed groups to collaborate on projects, such as crowd-sourced support to disaster relief. (Gourley, 2014) SaaS is useful for both monitoring and contributing to distributed activities.

SaaS is limited to only the software provided by the CSP. Users cannot bring their own software, and unlike PaaS, they can't bring their own code. While SaaS is the least flexible, it also provides the greatest economies of scale, providing the largest availability of a specified type of software to the largest group at the least cost. As usual, security concerns exist whenever working remotely and when working with others who may be unknown to you.

Other "X"aaS Variants

In addition to IaaS, PaaS and SaaS, niche variants to these three basic service models have appeared over time. In most cases, these have been created by CSPs to differentiate themselves from other CSPs. but these other variants also attempt to provide capabilities or overcome constraints in the vanilla service models.

For example, Desktop as a Service (DaaS) is a variant of SaaS. In DaaS, the CSP typically takes full responsibility for hosting and maintaining the compute, storage and access infrastructure, as well as applications and application software licenses needed to provide the desktop service, in return for a fixed monthly fee. The CSP may provide either persistent or non-persistent desktops, and usually the persistent ones are more expensive since they must be maintained even when idle. The primary advantage of DaaS is that the CSP provides everything the user will need to replicate an office-like environment, except for the organization's data.

Another SaaS variant is the Business Process as a Service (BPaaS). BPaaS provides access to business process software provided by the CSP.

A variant of PaaS is the Database as a Service (DBaaS). The CSP provides a database that users gain access to. The CSP handles all of the headaches of managing and backing up the database, while the user enters, analyzes and retrieves the desired data.

Note that this is not an exhaustive list of XaaS variants, and new variants appear fairly regularly over time.

Software Licenses on the Cloud

Who pays for the software licenses customers use on the various types of clouds? That depends on the type of cloud and the service level agreement.

For Storage Clouds, no software applications are running, so there is no licensing issue.

For IaaS clouds, the customer is renting the infrastructure, so whatever the customer has in terms of software licenses would be used on the VMs in the IaaS Type 2 Cloud. (See the software license agreement for what counts as a separate installation of the specific software package.)

For PaaS and SaaS clouds, the platform provider and the software provider own the licenses, and depending on the SLA, the user may pay a fee for the use of the platform or software. In a similar manner, in Desktop as a Service, the CSP owns the licenses and wraps up the cost of the software as part of their offering to the customer. The same applies to database as a service, where the service provider owns the license and offers access to the customers for a price.

Note that someone is always the owner of the software license and responsible for fulfilling the end user license agreement. The owner of the software may be the customer (i.e., bring your own software and its license) or it may be owned by the cloud service provider (who pays for the license and amortizes the cost across the customers).

Questions PMs Should Ask About Type 2 Clouds

Due to the range of Type 2 Cloud service models (IaaS, PaaS, SaaS and other variants), the different types of VMs that can be selected, the different responsibilities of the CSP versus the user, and different pricing options, there are a number of questions PMs should ask the CSPs about Type 2 Clouds. Some of these questions are:

- What is the cost of the data stored? A couple of years ago the answer was relatively straightforward, such as how many pennies per gigabyte stored per month, but now the pricing is often more complicated, requiring the use of online calculators from each CSP.

- How many and what type of VMs are available? Different CSPs provide different mixes of VMs, but most will provide the more common VM variants. In addition to the types of VMs, ask the CSP whether any particular VM configuration (of operating system and service pack) has been used operationally on this cloud, or whether you will be the first to use that configuration. If the VM configuration has not been tested previously, it may not work the first time as intended.

- What is the cost per time period for each type of VM? In 2013, the cost per VM was fairly straightforward, such as $0.65 per hour for a Windows 7 VM. However, there is now a wide range of VMs available, and the costs may range from $0.06 per hour for a low-end Linux VM to $4.60 per hour for an optimized high-end Linux VM. Your cost will depend on your computation needs. See Chapter 8 for additional details on cloud VM options and pricing.

- Is there a charge for bandwidth usage to and/or from the remote site? In some cases, there is no limit on the bandwidth for entering the data into the cloud, but a fairly hefty charge for bandwidth for outgoing data. In other cases, there are breakpoints for any bandwidth usage, often with a "free" level of bandwidth for low bandwidth users.

- Who pays for the software licenses? That depends on the type of cloud and the service level agreement (Chapter 8). For Storage Clouds, there are no software applications, so no licenses are involved. For IaaS, the customer renting the infrastructure is responsible for the licenses of any software applications it uses on the cloud. For SaaS and PaaS, the CSP owns the software licenses, and may attempt to recoup the license fee as part of their price to the user.

- How secure or private is my data at rest when stored in a third-party cloud? Each CSP provides a set of basic security features, while other security features are the responsibility of the user. Carefully examine both the security provided by the CSP and the security the user is responsible for to ensure that the total security provided is sufficient for your organization's needs. For example, if you want to store Personally Identifiable Information (PII) on the cloud, will the security protections provided by the CSP be sufficient (in addition to encrypting the PII data at rest)?

- If the CSP does not provide the security protections or availability promised in the service level agreement, is the recourse for the user sufficient to cover the data breach? For example, if the data breach costs your organization $150,000 and the compensation provided by the CSP is $15,000, then the recourse provided by the CSP is insufficient for your use.

- Can I test the security of the cloud before entering real data? Usually, if the user has contracted with a CSP for a virtual private cloud (VPC), the CSP will allow the user to perform penetration testing on the VMs in the VPC leased by the user. The user can then test for the security of the encryption to and from the cloud, the encryption at rest, user access controls on the data, and whether deleted data can be retrieved from memory. Note that the security features being tested are the responsibility of the user, not the CSP.

Additional questions specific to cloud security and availability will be discussed in Chapters 7 and 8 respectively.

Other questions users should ask themselves and not the CSP are:

- Will a Type 2 Cloud be useful for my Continuity of Operations Plan (COOP)? It might be, depending on whether the organization is already used to support remote operations, such as performing approved telework. If so, then the employees are already familiar with remote access, but even so, the organization should rehearse the COOP periodically to ensure the plan will actually work when implemented. For example, if the plan does not include a communications rerouting plan or a data duplication plan, then the access and data required for the COOP to succeed will not be available.

- Am I starting a new business with limited investment? If so, using a Type 2 Cloud might be able to minimize the investment in the Information Technology infrastructure to begin work.

Utility Clouds and the PMBOK® Guide

The PMBOK® Guide describes the process groups and the knowledge areas performed by the project manager. This section will discuss where Type 2 Clouds might be involved in the five process groups and the ten knowledge areas of project management. As with a Storage Cloud, if the PM's organization already has an ongoing service level agreement with a CSP, then many of the following considerations are likely covered in the organization's standard operating procedures (SOPs).

Process Groups:

Initiating Process Group:

During project initiation, the PM needs to determine whether a Type 2 Cloud is the best fit for the project (as opposed to a Type 1, Type 3, or no cloud), and if so, which of the service models (IaaS, PaaS, SaaS, or other variants) would best meet the needs of the project. What is the purpose for using a Type 2 Cloud and a particular service model? The use of a Type 2 Cloud may be mandated by the organization, or the use may be selected by the PM. The PM should develop a succinct description of why a Type 2 Cloud will be used and how it will be used on this project. In addition to why a certain service model was selected, indicating why the other service models were *not* selected can help explain the rationale of the selection. Ensure that the project stakeholders are not only identified, but also on board with the selection.

Planning Process Group:

If a Type 2 Cloud has been selected for use in this project, then a Type 2 Cloud service provider (CSP) will need to be selected during the planning phase (assuming the organization does not already have a standing agreement with a Type 2 Cloud CSP). If the use of a Storage Cloud to support a project is an innovation within your organization, then how the Type 2 Cloud will be used to support the existing or new business model will need to be described.

For example, if the PM selects an IaaS service model, then the PM needs to describe how the project will access, use and secure the data and operations at the remote CSP site, unless the organization already has SOPs for such use. Alternatively, if a PaaS or SaaS would meet the project's needs, then how the project members will leverage the selected capability will need to be described. (In the future, it is likely that Type 2 Cloud usage will be so familiar that using Type 2 Clouds will become the standard operating procedure.)

If the Type 2 Cloud will also be used as part of a Continuity of Operations Plan, then how the Type 2 Cloud will be accessed, used and secured during continuing operations should also be described.

Further planning will be required for determining how the data will be encrypted in transit and at rest on the Type 2 Cloud. Creating the access control list for who from each location has access to which data will also be important.

Risk planning will include assessing the risk of a data breach, and what to do if the data is temporarily unavailable from the CSP (such as due to a power failure). Risk planning should also consider whether the recourse provided by the CSP in the SLA is sufficient to cover the expected penalty to the project if such a risk is realized.

Executing Process Group:

If the PM's organization does not already include someone whose job will be to monitor the use of the cloud and the services provided by the CSP, then the PM will need to include someone on the project team with sufficient skills and resources to do so. In addition, the PM is responsible for the communications among all stakeholders, including the project team and the CSP, during execution.

Monitoring and Controlling Process Group:

The PM needs to monitor (or have someone monitor) the access control list to the Type 2 Cloud, as well as other key security monitoring activities. (See Chapter 7 for additional details on security monitoring procedures.) When employees terminate their employment, it is important to not only secure the physical and local network assets, but also secure the remote Type 2 Cloud assets from unauthorized access.

Other features to monitor are whether the use of the Type 2 Cloud is meeting the expected availability and performance guarantees, or whether there are problems with the efficiency of the system.   Making sure the CSP meets the criteria for availability as described in the service level agreement will also be important.   Periodically checking that the data being transmitted or at rest are actually encrypted is also a good business practice. Periodic penetration testing of your VPC (if applicable) is also useful.

The PM needs to ensure that the actual use and performance of the Type 2 Cloud matches the expectations as defined in the business model for the project. In addition, the PM needs to monitor and update project risks associated with using the Type 2 Cloud. (See the risk knowledge area below.)

Closing Process Group:

If the use of the Type 2 Cloud by your organization will continue beyond the end of the project, then the PM needs to ensure that the access control is correctly closed out. If the Type 2 Cloud will no longer be used at the end of the project, then the final disposition of the organization's software and data stored in the Type 2 Cloud will need to be addressed.

Knowledge Areas:

Stakeholder Management Knowledge Area:

The PM will need to determine which team members and other stakeholders will need access to the Utility Cloud. The types of access, types of VMs, types of applications, required response times, and required bandwidth will describe stakeholder needs and the type and quality of service required by the CSP. Business needs and constraints on who can access sensitive information and applications will determine which stakeholders obtain which types of accesses. The PM needs to ensure through the stakeholder engagement plan the needs and expectations of the stakeholders, as well as whether those needs and expectations are being met throughout the project.

Communications Knowledge Area:

Communications to stakeholders should include how the Type 2 Cloud will be used to support the project. In addition, the PM needs to prepare the plan for how secure access to and transmission of the data to and from the cloud will be ensured and monitored during the project. (This is assuming that the organization does not already have in place standard operating procedures for communicating with a remote cloud.)

Risk Knowledge Area:

Before selecting a Type 2 Cloud, list and evaluate the risks of using a Type 2 Cloud of the particular service model selected for this project. This risk assessment should be performed even if third-party clouds have become standard operating procedure for the PM's organization. After selecting the Type 2 Cloud, monitor the access, communications and data stored in the cloud for any changes in the risk factors. Also consider any risks associated with the closing out of the project in terms of data remaining in the cloud or transitioning data location or changes in access to the data at project closeout.

Procurement Knowledge Area:

Procurement of a Type 2 Cloud service level agreement (SLA) is a prerequisite to using a Type 2 Cloud for any service model. See Chapter 8 for additional details related to SLAs. If the PM's organization has an SLA in place with a CSP, this is less of an issue.

Cost Knowledge Area:

The use of a Type 2 Cloud will entail a cost that must be planned and managed. Delegation of authority for who can increase the type and number of VMs, storage space or bandwidth would be a good cost control tool to consider.

Integration Knowledge Area:

The use of a Type 2 Cloud must be integrated into the organization's business model. How will it be used? Will the offsite Type 2 Cloud resources be used in conjunction with onsite information technology resources, and if so, how? What will the Type 2 Cloud be used for? Who will have access to the data and why? How long will the data be stored before being aged off? How will on-site and remote data be kept in sync (if both are being used on the project)? If the Type 2 Cloud will be used as part of a continuity of operations plan, how will it be used and how will you train for it? As stated above, these questions assume that use of a Type 2 Cloud is not already part of your organization's SOPs.

Scope Knowledge Area:

How will the Type 2 Cloud be used within your business model? What will the cloud not be used for? Which types of data will be stored in the cloud and which will not? How many VMs, how much storage, and how much bandwidth will be used in the Type 2 Cloud each month? If the scope of use changes over time, how will that scope creep be managed? It will also be useful to monitor whether the project is actually using the Type 2 Cloud and selected service model as planned, or whether team members are working around unanticipated issues.

Time Knowledge Area:

When will operations be transitioned to start using a Type 2 Cloud? (This again assumes that using Type 2 Clouds is not standard for your organization.) Or for a particular project, when will the project start using the Type 2 Cloud as part of its operations? Are all stakeholders on board with the timing of the use of the Type 2 Cloud? Is the cloud service provider on-board with the transition time, the anticipated number of VMs, storage and bandwidth required, access controls, encryption, and penetration testing (if applicable)? Are the latency (response times) of getting data to or from the cloud within the time frames specified by the SLA?

Quality Knowledge Area:

What is the Type 2 Cloud availability, and does it match the SLA? What is the performance of the VMs, and do they match expectations? What is the latency for data upload, access and download, and does it match the SLA? How is the quality of service measured according to the SLA? Who in the project or organization will monitor the performance of the Storage Cloud provider and how?

Human Resources Knowledge Area:

There are no specific human resource requirements for using a CSP's Utility Clouds.

Chapter 6:
Type 3 Cloud:
Data-Focused Cloud

Overview

The first section of this chapter describes the Type 3 or Data-focused Cloud, how it works, and how it differs from Type 1 and Type 2 Clouds. (Note that details of using map-reduce programs to analyze data in files stored in Type 3 Clouds will be described in Chapter 9.)

The second section describes the difference between *structured* data and *unstructured* data, and how the Type 3 Cloud handles both types.

The third section describes what a Data-focused Cloud can do for your project given the preceding definitions.

The fourth section compares traditional relational database form and function to data stored in Cloud Table format. The various table formats in cloud computing define a mental model that is different from traditional database structures and queries. It is important for PMs to understand this new mental model as a prerequisite for any projects with Data-focused Cloud to succeed.

The fifth section presents the advantages and disadvantages of Data-focused Clouds, including the time required to run map-reduce programs compared to traditional relational database queries.

The sixth section presents a set of questions PMs should ask with respect to Data-focused Clouds.

The last section presents the project management process groups and knowledge areas of the PMBOK® Guide as they relate to Type 3 Clouds.

The Data-Focused Cloud

The third type of cloud is the Data-focused Cloud. The purpose of a Data-focused Cloud is to run Big Data parallel processing programs (or analytics) on huge data sets. These huge data sets are larger than previously accessible data sets, for reasons described later.

The current NIST definition of Big Data includes the following points:

- Big Data refers to the *inability* of traditional data architectures to efficiently handle new data sets [italics added].

- Big Data consists of extensive datasets, primarily in the characteristics of volume, velocity, and/or variety that require a scalable architecture for efficient storage, manipulation, and analysis.

- The Big Data paradigm consists of the distribution of data systems across horizontally coupled, independent resources to achieve the scalability needed for the efficient processing of extensive datasets. (NIST Big Data, 2014)

Note that traditional data architectures are unable to handle the new data sets of Big Data. The Data-focused Cloud is designed to handle these new data sets in a horizontal or parallel manner.

Moreover, these Big Data analytics can be run on commodity hardware (cheap, identical hard drives and processors) rather than the specialized hardware previously used to perform parallel computing. Prior to Data-focused Clouds, large-scale parallel processing required specialized computing machines called high-performance computing (HPC) platforms. Any programs you wanted run on an HPC required reprogramming your software into parallel processing software that ran on specialized machines with many parallel computing nodes. The user had to not only rewrite the program, but also had to handle which code segments and which data went to which nodes and when, and then handle the load balancing over time so that one node wouldn't be swamped while other nodes remained idle. Writing and running of programs on HPCs was more of an art than a science. As a result, a number of niche programs, such as "finite element" programs that simulated things like explosions and wind tunnels, were common types of programs run on HPCs.

What Type 3 Clouds provide is a relatively inexpensive and more straightforward approach to parallel processing. *The Data-focused Cloud provides parallel processing for the masses.* Anyone who can write a Type 3 Cloud program (called a map reduce program for reasons described later) can run large-scale parallel processing programs that were previously unavailable except to a few. The Hadoop framework handles which nodes are used, where the data is located, how to move data around and duplicate it when necessary, monitors load balancing, and monitors the progress of the parallel programs for the user. All the user needs to know is how to write a map-reduce program (described later), and the Hadoop framework handles the rest.

According to Wikipedia:

Apache Hadoop is an open source software framework for storage and large-scale processing of data sets on clusters of commodity hardware. Hadoop is an Apache top-level project being built and used by a global community of contributors and users. (Wikipedia, "Apache Hadoop", 2013)

So Apache Hadoop is an open-source project, and the Hadoop framework contains four main modules (also from same reference):

- *Hadoop Common* — contains libraries and utilities needed by other Hadoop modules

- *Hadoop Distributed File System (HDFS)* — a distributed file-system that stores data on commodity machines, providing very high aggregate bandwidth across the cluster.

- *Hadoop YARN* — a resource-management platform responsible for managing compute resources in clusters and using them for scheduling of users' applications.

- *Hadoop MapReduce* — a programming model for large scale data processing.

This book will focus only on the Hadoop Distributed File System (HDFS) and the Hadoop MapReduce programming model. (You would only need to know about the Hadoop Common libraries and the Hadoop YARN scheduler if you were running map-reduce programs yourself.)

Note that the term Hadoop has been used to describe many functions, so that the term now tends to have specific modifiers to distinguish the various uses of elements of Hadoop:

- Apache Hadoop is an open source project

- Hadoop Framework contains four modules (listed below)

- Hadoop Distributed File System (HDFS) manages your structured and unstructured data files on a cluster of commodity machines (i.e., a cloud)

- Hadoop MapReduce is the parallel processing programming language for Big Data

- Hadoop YARN manages resources and helps schedule user applications

- Hadoop Common contains the libraries and utilities called by all of the other elements

When someone mentions "Hadoop," it is important that you both know which context they are using.

The Type 3 Cloud differs from the Type 1 Cloud and the Type 2 Cloud as shown in Figure 6.1. While a Type 3 Cloud also uses lots of (commodity) hardware of the same type, the wide range of VMs available on a Type 2 Cloud are neither present nor desired on a Type 3 Cloud. Early on, the Hadoop Distributed File System (HDFS) was installed on VMs and the Hadoop map-reduce programs were run on top, but it was found that the performance could be dramatically improved by installing the HDFS directly on the hard drives running a UNIX-based operating system. (See OpenStack's Sahara Project for an exception where HDFS is running on VMs.) (Sahara, 2014) So instead of having lots of memory with VMs running on the processors, the Type 3 Cloud has lots of memory with the Hadoop Distributed File System installed and Hadoop map-reduce programs running on top.

There is another parallel processing framework that was developed by the Open Cloud Consortium (http://opencloud consortium.org) called Sector, but it has not gained the popularity and widespread adoption of Hadoop. We will focus only on Hadoop for the remainder of this book.

Cloud Type 1: Storage Cloud	Lots of Memory			
Cloud Type 2: Utility Cloud	Lots of Memory	+	Virtual Machines	
→ Cloud Type 3: A Data-focused Cloud	Lots of Memory	+	Hadoop Distributed File System	+ Hadoop ← Map-reduce

**Figure 6.1: How the Type 3 Cloud Differs from
Type 1 or Type 2 Clouds**

Structured and Unstructured Data

Structured data is data that is represented in some format that allows it to be stored and queried in a database. More formally, "Data that resides in a fixed field within a record or file is called structured data. This includes data contained in relational databases and spreadsheets." (Beal, 2014)

Unstructured data is defined by the same source as "information that doesn't reside in a traditional row-column database."   More generally, Wikipedia defines unstructured data as "Information that either does not have a pre-defined data model or is not organized in a predefined manner."   (Wikipedia, "Unstructured Data," 2014) Unstructured data is generally stored as text files, but these files may also include numbers, dates, web pages, or even binary data.

The good news is that the Type 3 Cloud can handle both structured and unstructured data, and can be used to turn most unstructured data into structured data. Figure 6.2 shows how legacy structured data and unstructured data can be manipulated in a Data-focused Cloud.

Starting in the top left of Figure 6.2, structured data is stored in a legacy relational database, such as Microsoft Access or Oracle or even a spreadsheet. As will be described later in this chapter, the existing structured data in a legacy database can be readily translated into a structured data model in some form of Table that can be stored in HDFS. Three types of Tables used in clouds (as will be described both in this chapter and Chapter 9) are:

- Triple stores (RDF or Resource Data Format)
- Big Table (a five-tuple store), and
- Accumulo (a six-tuple store)

This chapter will focus on the RDF triple store as the way to most easily understand what's different about Type 3 Clouds, and then focus on structured data in Accumulo table format.

Accumulo calls an entire data set a "table," while subsets of the whole data set are called "tablets." Tablets are very useful in Accumulo because it allows for more efficient parallel processing of the entire data set (or table) by placing subsets (tablets) of the data on different processing nodes.

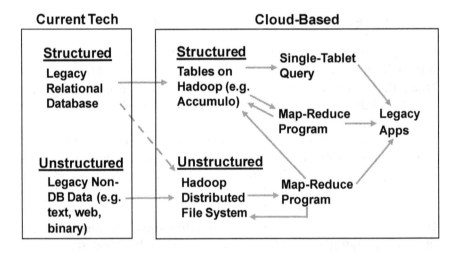

Figure 6.2: Type 3 Clouds Handle Both Structured and Unstructured Data

Once the structured data is stored in Accumulo, then a map-reduce program can be run against an Accumulo table, which automatically runs the program against multiple tablets. (Note that Accumulo also has a set of "Java calls" that search more like a traditional relational data base query. For example, if one queries for a specific ID, Accumulo automatically finds the right tablet and returns the applicable Accumulo rows.)

The outputs from either the query or map-reduce program can

then be stored in any legacy application or format, including text, spreadsheets, or other relational databases. Outputs of map-reduce programs run against Accumulo can also be stored as Accumulo tables instead of legacy applications.

Conversely, starting in the lower left of Figure 6.2, one can instead start with legacy unstructured data and place whole files directly into the cloud, where it is stored, replicated (for redundancy purposes) and searchable within the Hadoop Distributed File System. Hadoop map-reduce programs are then run against these files of unstructured data, and the outputs of the map-reduce programs can be sent directly to legacy applications (as described above), or placed in an Accumulo structured data format, or even returned as new files to the Hadoop Distributed File System for further processing.

It is not uncommon to run overnight a large map-reduce program on unstructured data and then store the structured data output in Accumulo for users to access the next morning. The users may then run a more focused map-reduce program on the data in the Accumulo tablets produced by the overnight run. The actual runtime is dependent on many factors, including the size of the whole data set and how many processing nodes are available.

Note the dotted line in Figure 6.2. This arrow represents the fact that one could take the legacy structured data and place it as unstructured data in the Hadoop Distributed File System. While less common, it may be useful to throw a disparate set of databases together and see what the map-reduce program can find in terms of relationships from these various data sources, regardless of how the data was previously organized. Usually, however, legacy databases are translated into one of the table formats in a Data-focused Cloud.

What Data-Focused Clouds Can Do For You

Data-focused Clouds allow users to store and analyze *huge* amounts of structured and unstructured non-relational data. By huge we mean petabytes or larger amounts of data. What's a petabyte? (No, it's not a dog that bites you when you pet it.) A petabyte is 1,000,000,000,000,000 bytes of data. (That's a one followed by 15 zeros.) As a basis of comparison, a 2000 study by Lyman and Varian estimated the uncompressed textual data in its 26 million books in the Library of Congress to contain 10 terabytes of data, or one percent of a petabyte. (Lyman and Varian, 2000) See Table 6.1 for the various magnitudes of data (excerpted from Wikipedia, "Petabyte," 2014).

Note that the addressing scheme of most traditional relational databases would not reach or exceed a petabyte of data. Therefore, even if one could stuff over a petabyte of data into most legacy relational databases, one couldn't access it because it would extend beyond the known addressing mechanism. Cloud computing not only allows the ability to locate and retrieve data from more than petabytes of data, it allows anyone with basic knowledge of map-reduce programming and access to a Type 3 Cloud the ability to search and analyze petabytes or more of data. This is empowering. For those who claim "there is nothing new about cloud computing," the ability to allow almost anyone the ability to store and analyze petabytes of data is, by itself, a new thing.

Table 6.1: Magnitudes of Data Storage

Number of Bytes	Name	Abbreviation
1000	kilobyte	kB
1000^2	megabyte	MB
1000^3	gigabyte	GB
1000^4	terabyte	TB
1000^5	petabyte	PB
1000^6	exabyte	EB
1000^7	zettabyte	ZB
1000^8	yottabyte	YB

One reason that Data-focused Clouds provide "parallel processing for the masses" is that the Hadoop framework (defined above) handles all of the overhead associated with storing, locating, and processing your data. The user does not need to worry about load balancing, or even where the data is located. The Hadoop framework automatically parallelizes the elements of the program and farms out the "map" part of the map-reduce program to the various nodes where the data is located. It then returns the data already sorted to the "reduce" part of the map-reduce program, which then either sums up the desired numbers, or provides the list of responses requested by the program. It is also common for map-reduce programs to be run to extract a desired subset of the unstructured data so that further processing of the returned subset of data takes less time.

Not only does the Hadoop framework manage the parallel processing, it also manages data storage and replication. As described in Chapter 4, the data in a cloud using HDFS is automatically replicated to ensure data is not lost. HDFS ensures that the original and two copies of the data (for a total of three copies) are made when the data is first ingested or whenever any new data created by a map-reduce program is stored in HDFS. In addition, HDFS makes sure that one of the copies is not even in the same rack in case there is a catastrophic disaster. HDFS also allows the ability to store and manipulate files larger than the standard memory block size, and has built-in data compression options. The user does not have to worry about any of this behind-the-scenes book keeping—it is all handled by HDFS. This gives people with far fewer data processing skills far more access to parallel processing than in the past.

Because Data-focused Clouds can store and allow parallel processing of huge amounts of data, users are more readily able to find relationships among a wide range of data sources that were previously undiscovered. For example, as shown in a TV ad, someone was able to find the relationship between which types of baked goods were purchased from bakeries depending on the weather. On sunny days, more people tended to buy sandwiches, while on wet days, people tended to buy more cake. Since bakeries don't like to bake and then discard what doesn't sell, getting insight as to what will sell on a given day given the weather forecast can be a significant cost saver for a bakery. (IBM, "Meteolytix," 2011)

This is just one example of many such useful correlations discovered by using Type 3 Clouds for Big Data analysis. (More examples are described in Chapter 9.) In general, Big Data is considered to include anywhere from hundreds of terabytes to many petabytes of data in a single data set. In 2012, Gartner defined Big Data as "high volume, high velocity, and/or high variety information assets that require new forms of processing to enable enhanced decision making, insight discovery and process optimization." (Wikipedia, "Big Data," 2014)

In addition to being able to process large amounts of data, a Data-focused Cloud also allows users to be able to add new types of data without having to (necessarily) change the map-reduce parallel processing programs or single-tablet queries. While traditional relational databases require the addition of new columns and new rows, Type 3 Clouds simply "tack on" the new data, and HDFS has no problem finding the new data using map-reduce programs. Why this is so is described in the next section.

Comparing Data-Focused Clouds to Traditional Relational Databases and Queries

Since all learning involves comparing and contrasting something new to something you already know, we will start by describing a sample problem using traditional relational database format, then translate it into a cloud-based table format. For ease of understanding, we will first demonstrate mapping a legacy relational database into a triple-store, and then into an Accumulo six-tuple store.

Relational Database Format

Relational databases usually consist of rows and columns, as in a spreadsheet. Figure 6.3 shows a relational database of rows and columns. In this example, each row represents a particular person, while each column represents the attributes of that person. The row header is the person's name, while the column headers are the person's address, age, and height. There may be many more attributes, and each would have its own column header. One row exists for each person, and there can be many, many rows of data.

The highlighting in this example represents a query being run against this relational database. As shown in the bottom of the figure, the query is set to "find the names of those persons more than 25 years of age but less than 60 years of age, and more than five feet tall." The result is highlighted in bold-italic text, while the query criteria are shown in just bold text. In this example within the table, we have highlighted those criteria that were met by both conditions (age and height) and selected the names of those that meet those criteria.

Relational databases work well when the database if densely populated—that is, most of the elements in the row-column format have data in them. In addition, relational database format performs very well when only the number of rows changes (i.e., new entries are added but the information collected about each entry remains the same). When the number of columns change, the relational database is said to be changing its "data model." This means that previous queries need to be adapted to the fact that there are now additional columns in the database not previously there.

Name	Address	Age	Height	•••
John Smith	Washington DC	**35**	**5'10"**	
Jane Doe	Baltimore	**29**	**5'8"**	
Fred Flintstone	Rockville	55	4'10"	
Tony D. Tiger	Battle Creek	67	6'2"	
Elmer Fudd	DeForest	60	4'6"	
Peter Parker	New York	**28**	**5'5"**	
Bruce Wayne	Gotham	**36**	**6'1"**	
Roger Rabbit	Fantasyland	41	4'0"	
Peter Rabbit	Rural Address	118	1'1"	
White Rabbit	Wonderland	135	1'11"	

⋮   Find the **Names** of those of **Age >25 but <60, and > 5' tall**

Figure 6.3: Sample Relational Database and Query Example

Type 3 Clouds represent and store the data in a different format. That format doesn't care whether the database is densely or sparsely populated. Moreover, you can add as many different data types as you like without having to change the data model or the queries. We will explain how this works first by showing how the raw data might appear in disparate databases before being placed in table format, then placing the data into a triple store format, and then showing how the data can be represented in an Accumulo format.

Figure 6.4 shows three different hypothetical data sets: medical records, social media, and a dating service. Note that some of the data shown in Figure 6.3 appears in Figure 6.4. The representation of data from disparate data sources could be placed into traditional relational database format, but this would need to be done manually, or by having a program written to ingest and map each unique data source into the format in Figure 6.3. The data model from each of the disparate data sources must be mapped to the data model of the desired relational database. Note that the query criteria is in bold and the resulting names are in bold italic in Figure 6.4, just as they were in Figure 6.3.

Medical Records	Social Media	Dating Service
John Smith	*John Smith*	
Age 35 5'10"	Washington DC	
810 K Street		
	Peter Parker	*Peter Parker*
	Age 28	5'5"
		New York
Bruce Wayne	*Bruce Wayne*	
Gotham	36 6'1"	

Find the **Names** of those of **Age >25 but <60, and > 5' tall** from multiple data sets

Figure 6.4: Sample Disparate Data Sets to be Placed in Cloud Table Format

Triple Store Format Example

Type 3 Clouds provide an alternative way to store structured data from a traditional relational database. We will first describe how to place data in Resource Data Format (RDF), and then show how to translate any relational database into RDF format.

In RDF, rather than having a set of rows and columns, each element from the disparate data sources is represented by a "triple store." An RDF triple consists of a subject, a predicate, and an object as shown in Figure 6.5.   For example, the first column is some identifier for all of the records related to this person, while the second column represents some attribute of the person, such as the person's name. The third column is the actual name of the person associated with that attribute.

Compare the first six rows of Figure 6.5 to the upper left of Figure 6.4. Note that for every element of data in the disparate data sources in Figure 6.4, there is one row in triple store format in Figure 6.5.

Row (Subject)	Attribute (Predicate)	Value (Object)
001	Name	*John Smith*
001	Age	**35**
001	Height	**5' 10"**
001	City	Wash DC
001	Street	K Street
001	Number	810
002	Name	*Peter Parker*
002	Age	**28**
002	Height	**5' 5"**
002	City	New York

Note: No street number or street name for Peter Parker

⋮ Find the **Names** of those of **Age >25 but <60, and > 5' tall**

Figure 6.5: Sample Triple Store Constructed from Disparate Data Sources

Now compare the first six rows of Figure 6.5 to the first row of Figure 6.3. All of the data elements for John Smith in the first row of Figure 6.3 are represented in the RDF format of the first six rows of Figure 6.5. This provides the translation from data in traditional relational databases into a more cloud-friendly format for structured data. This is also why it is relatively straightforward to transfer data from traditional relational databases to structured data in cloud tables.

Once again, to highlight this key point, remember that *any legacy relational database can be translated into cloud table-structured data format.* Figure 6.6 shows an example of this commonly used mapping from legacy relational databases into a Data-focused Cloud-based data format. This is one reason why Data-focused Cloud computing has become popular—it is relatively straightforward and automatable for translating data from relational databases into a table format.

	Column 1	Column 2	Col. 3	Col. 4
	Name	**Address**	**Age**	**Height**
Row 1	*John Smith*	Washington DC	35	5'10"
Row 2	*Jane Doe*	Baltimore	29	5'8"
Row 3	Fred Flintstone	Rockville	55	4'10"

Relational Database

RDF

Row (Subject)	Column (Predicate)	Value (Object)
001	Name	*John Smith*
001	Address	Washington DC
001	Age	**35**
001	Height	5'10"
002	Name	*Jane Doe*
002	Address	Baltimore

Figure 6.6: Sample Mapping of Legacy Relational Database into Triple Store Format

In Figure 6.6, for the relational database in the upper left, the first row and first column (Name) element is John Smith. In the triple store in the lower right:

- The first row first column (Subject) is identified with an ID number (001) to correspond with the first row of the relational database,

- The second column is the (Predicate) attribute called Name based on the relational database first column header, and

- The value (Object) is John Smith, which is the cell element in the relational database.

Each element in a relational database has a clear mapping to each row in the triple store list. If all your legacy data comes from the same relational database, then the translation will be easy. If, instead, you are combining data from multiple legacy databases, then a disambiguation step is required to ensure that all of the data associated with "John Smith" belongs to the same John Smith.

Also note that this doesn't address any unstructured legacy data your organization may have; unstructured data will be covered in

Chapter 9. One key feature of Type 3 Clouds is that they can let organizations analyze both their structured and unstructured data.

If one can translate data in relational databases into triple store format, why bother? There are several reasons. First, one advantage of the triple store is that it acts like one long list. As more data is added, it is simply tacked onto the end of the list. No new columns ever need to be defined. This becomes an important prerequisite to allowing parallel computing via map-reduce programs.

The raw data source format doesn't matter to the triple store format. Just map every element of the data in its raw form into a new row in the triple store format. It doesn't matter whether there are one, two, or fifty different data formats in legacy databases; they can all be translated into one really long list in triple store format.

Benefits of Triple Store Format

Note that the data model never needs to change, because the data models of the legacy databases are already absorbed into the RDF table format. And since the data model never changes, any existing cloud table queries can be run because attributes (predicates) that are new and not yet included in the queries are simply ignored. Moreover, both old and new queries can be run against the data in triple store format without needing to change anything.

The primary concern of combining disparate legacy databases is the need to make sure that the subject is actually the same between the disparate databases. For example, is the John Smith from the medical records the same John Smith in social media? This disambiguation step can take some time, but one only has to do that once per new database. If one relied on traditional queries of multiple databases, that disambiguation would have to occur each time the separate queries were run on different databases.

For example, if John H. Smith has identifier 001, then every data element (row) in the triple store about John Smith should carry the same identifier (001). However, a different John Smith (say John W. Smith) and all of it associated data elements should have a different identifier (such as 002).

If one were to try and combine all disparate legacy relational databases into a single huge relational database, the result would likely be a "sparse" data set. That is, there would be a large number of rows with only a few elements filled under each column. For example, if there were 10 data sets each with 5 unique column headers and 100 unique rows of data, then the combined data set would be 50 columns wide (5 columns x 10 data sets) and 1000 rows in length (100 rows x 10 data sets). Of these 50,000 possible data elements (50 columns x1000 rows), only 5,000 elements would have data (10 data sets times 5 columns by 100 rows). That means only 10% of the relational database would have data and the remaining 90% would be empty.

Rather than build a large row-and-column relational database that will be mostly empty, translate the data from a row-and-column format into a list, where each row in the list is the data that describes each cell with data. Each cell can be represented by an RDF triple store as described above. Continuing our previous example, the RDF representation would have 15,000 elements (5,000 unique data items, where each data item requires a subject, predicate and object as the triple store for each unique data item). An RDF representation of as a "list" of data elements is much more efficient than a 50,000 cell matrix that only has data in 5,000 cells. Note that the real benefits of the RDF triple store increases as the size and variety of the original data increases.

Medical Records	Facebook	Dating Service	Drivers Licenses (New Data Source Added with New Format)
John Smith Age 35 5'10"	*John Smith* Washington DC		
			Jane Doe Age 29 5'8" Baltimore 666 Sycamore St.
	Peter Parker Age 28	*Peter Parker* 5'5" New York	*Peter Parker* 777 5th Ave. New York
Bruce Wayne Gotham	*Bruce Wayne* 36 6'1"		

Find the *Names* of those of **Age >25 but <60, and > 5' tall** from multiple data sets

Figure 6.7: Adding a New Data Source to Sample Disparate Data Sets

To continue our previous example, Figure 6.7 shows the raw data sources of Figure 6.4 but with the new data source of "Drivers Licenses" added. Figure 6.8 then shows this same new data added to the "list" of triple store data previously shown in Figure 6.5. Not only was Jane Doe's name, age, height, city and street added to the list, Peter Parker's street address was also added to the list. None of the previous data about Peter parker needed to change, only a new entry was added to the list. Note that adding new rows to the list doesn't change the triple store format—it just adds rows to the list.

Row (Subject)	Attribute (Predicate)	Value (Object)
002	Name	*Peter Parker*
002	Age	**28**
002	Height	**5' 5"**
002	Address	777 5th Ave.
002	City	New York
003	Name	*Jane Doe*
003	Age	**35**
003	Height	**5' 8"**
003	City	Baltimore
003	Street	Sycamore Street
003	Number	666

⋮

Find the **Names** of those of **Age >25 but <60, and > 5' tall**

Figure 6.8: New Data Source Added to Rows in Triple Store Format

In reality, we know that the list of triple store data cannot be infinitely long, and that it wouldn't be efficient to start at the top and go through the whole list every time one runs a query. That's where parallel processing comes in. The triple store lends itself to parallel processing because the long list can be separated into smaller lists, and *then the exact same query can be run separately on each part of the list.*

This is another important distinction between relational databases and triple stores. Because the triple store format is the same for every part of the list, each part of the list can be placed on a separate node. (These portions of lists are actually called tablets in Accumulo.) Then, the exact same query can be sent to each node, and each node will process the query and return the results. (One actually runs map-reduce programs instead of queries across multiple tablets, but we will describe how that works in Chapter 9.)

Note that the triple store has been around since 1999. (Wikipedia, "Resource Description Framework," 2014) However, the creation of Data-focused Clouds has made this infinitely extensible list-type data structure much more useful for solving Big Data problems. As described above, Hadoop Distributed File System (HDFS) handles all of the overhead of parallel processing. Thus, once the data in legacy relational databases has been placed into a cloud-based data table, such as a triple store, then the power of parallel processing can be brought to bear much more easily than in the past.

Accumulo Format

The RDF triple store format is not the only type of format compatible to cloud computing. Google uses Big Table format, which is actually a five-tuple instead of a triple store. In addition to the same basic three elements of a triple store, the Big Table format has two more columns that are used to assist in making queries faster. This book will not describe Big Tables further, other than to say that all of the benefits of triple store apply to Big Table format, and there are additional performance benefits obtained by using the additional column qualifiers to speed up queries.

Accumulo is another Data-focused Cloud format that uses a six-tuple to store its data. Accumulo uses the same three triple store columns, uses one column qualifier like Big Tables, but then adds two new columns, as shown in Figure 6.9.

The first new column is the "time" stamp, which usually represents the time the data in this row was entered into the table format. The time stamp is very useful in determining which entry is the most recent. This is essential when a user wants to view only the most recent entry for any related data item.

Note that Data-focused Clouds tend to just keep *adding* data, rather than finding previously entered data and changing it. This is because it takes *40 times as long* to seek, find, and change an existing entry than it does to just write a new row entry. (Hoff, 2009) Therefore, the Accumulo tablet that tracks the address of John Smith as shown in Figure 6.9 would have a new row added at the end with John Smith's new address and a more recent time stamp than the old entry. A user wanting to retrieve data from this tablet would specify that only the most recent data be displayed. The time stamp is also often used to batch process the available data and "age off" and delete or archive data past a certain age.

The second new column in Accumulo is the "security" column for access control. This column is used to control who gets to see the data in that specific row. In Figure 6.9, the data is marked PII for Personally Identifiable Information. PII must be protected from unauthorized access. So if the user access control system states that User A has access to PII, then User A will be able to see data in rows marked PII. Conversely, if User B is not approved by the access control system to see PII data, the user will not see any data in a row with the security stamp set to PII.

ID	Col. Family	Col. Qualifier	Time	Security	Value
001	Personal	Name	31 Apr '12	PII	*John Smith*
001	Personal	Age	31 Apr '12	PII	**35**
001	Personal	Height	31 Apr '12	PII	**5' 10"**
001	Address	City	31 Apr '12	PII	Wash DC
001	Address	Street	31 Apr '12	PII	K Street
001	Address	Number	31 Apr '12	PII	810
002	Personal	Name	31 Apr '12	PII	*Peter Parker*
002	Personal	Age	31 Apr '12	PII	28
002	Personal	Height	31 Apr '12	PII	**5' 5"**
002	Address	City	31 Apr '12	PII	New York
003	Personal	Name	31 Apr '12	PII	*Jane Doe*
003	Personal	Age	31 Apr '12	PII	29

Find the **Names** of those of **Age >25 but <60, and > 5' tall**

**Figure 6.9: Same Example in Accumulo
Six-tuple Data Format**

In practice, many factors need to be considered when allowing access to a given row. For example, one may require that the person having access to the PII data be "an employee, and works in Human Resources, and has PII access authorized." As a result, the security stamp often contains a very long Boolean (containing "and" and "or" expressions) so that the organization can fine-tune just who can see which rows of data. Accumulo designers go to great lengths to try to make the security stamp string variable all "and" statements so that the comparison of the user credential is easily compared to the required access as defined by the security stamp.

Accumulo was originally developed for the National Security Agency, but the NSA decided to release the Accumulo code to the Open Source community to help increase the speed of Accumulo development and make the benefits of the six-tuple approach available to the public. (Wikipedia, "Apache Accumulo," 2014) Accumulo is now another open source project under Apache, as is Hadoop.

One last point to be aware of about data in Accumulo table format: If one wants to query a single large Accumulo tablet, that single tablet query is called a "direct access table based search." Note that if the data you seek is stored on multiple Accumulo tablets, then it is more efficient to run a map-reduce program to find the desired data. The reason for this is simple. Map-reduce programs are parallel processing programs, while database queries are sequential, even in Accumulo. Note that the output of map-reduce programs run against Accumulo can be sent to Accumulo, as shown in Figure 6.2.

Advantages and Disadvantages of Data-Focused Clouds

The primary advantage of Data-focused Clouds is that anyone with access to data in a Type 3 Cloud can perform Big Data analysis with just knowledge of map-reduce programming. Type 3 Data-focused Clouds have made massively parallel data processing available to a much broader swath of society. No longer is parallel processing the exclusive realm of specialized high-performance computers. Big Data analysis performed on Type 3 Clouds really does provide parallel processing for the masses.

Type 3 Clouds also provide the opportunity for Big Data analysis. Huge data sets of hundreds of terabytes to dozens of petabytes are now common. Due to the parallel processing nature of Data-focused Clouds, the sizes of data sets to be analyzed can exceed the previous limitation of database addressing schemes. As shown in the previous bakery-weather correlation example, relationships among data elements can be discovered that were not previously known.

A third advantage of Type 3 Clouds is that they allow the storage and parallel processing analysis of both structured and unstructured data. Although this chapter focused on structured data analysis, Data-focused Clouds also perform Big Data analysis of unstructured data, as described in Chapter 9.

A fourth advantage of Type 3 Clouds is that anyone with legacy structured data relational database format can translate it directly into cloud-based triple stores (RDF), five-tuple stores (Big Tables), or six-tuple stores (Accumulo). Except for the need to perform disambiguation between similar data elements, this translation from legacy to cloud-based databases can be automated.

A fifth advantage of Type 3 Clouds is that additional new databases with different data models can be constantly added to the cloud-based data. This is because the Data-focused Clouds don't care what the original data model or format was, as long as it can be entered into one of the three-, five- or six-tuple formats. Moreover, the existing queries and map-reduce programs in the Type 3 Cloud do not need to be modified when the new data is added. New queries and map-reduce programs may need to be created to exploit the new types of data, but the old queries or map-reduce programs won't "break" due to the addition of the new data.

Overall, Type 3 Clouds (Data-focused Clouds) are useful:

- When you have huge data sets
- If your data can't be managed in a relational database (such as too large to address or too sparse to be efficient)
- If you are not sure what types of queries you want to run or relationships you want to discover
- If you want to perform parallel processing and combine the results of many independent processes run in parallel

Conversely, here are some circumstances when Type 3 Clouds are not useful:

- If you can answer all of your organization's questions with an existing relational database in a reasonable amount of time, why bother with the overhead of a cloud?

- If you need quick-response data analysis, and can't afford to wait for the results of an overnight map-reduce program run, you probably want an alternative processing approach. (Not all map-reduce programs take a long time to run, but many map-reduce programs do take many hours to complete depending on the amount of data being processed, how the data is being processed, and the number and speed of computation nodes available.)

- If you need to perform a seek, find, and replace function in your database (as opposed to write new and select only the most recent), then you probably want to use a traditional relational database.

- If your data can fit within an existing relational database and the queries you plan to run are fairly well defined, then you probably don't need a Type 3 Cloud.

Note that the projected magnitude of the data that needs to be processed is a key consideration (as are the velocity and variability described above in the definition of Big Data in the beginning of this chapter). In one seminar, an attendee mentioned that his customer was going to reach a petabyte of data in the next six months. This is the type of situation in which it would be appropriate to take the time and expend the effort to transfer the legacy data into one of the cloud data formats, and plan for the new business processes necessary to incorporate the use of a Type 3 Cloud.

Conversely, another attendee had a customer who was concerned that they might reach 5 terabytes of data by the following year. Since five terabytes of data is readily manageable by legacy relational databases, and since the customer did not expect the magnitude to grow significantly after that, the customer could just as easily choose to stay with their traditional relational database.

Questions PMs Should Ask About Type 3 Clouds

The first question a PM should ask is "Does this project need to use a Type 3 Cloud?" Assuming that your organization is not already using a Type 3 Cloud in its normal daily operations, the decision of whether or not to use a Data-focused Cloud depends on the type of project, its objectives and constraints. For example, if the project involves less than 100 terabytes of data and the existing legacy relational database can handle all the project's processing requirements, then the project probably doesn't need to use a cloud.

However, there may also be project-independent reasons for using a Data-focused Cloud, such as when the sponsor or higher management in your organization requires the use of a Type 3 Cloud.

There may be legitimate reasons to use a Type 3 Cloud on a project that could be accomplished without one; for example, the organization might wish to learn how using a Data-focused Cloud works on a smaller project, less complex project (that could be cross-checked using a legacy relational database) before embarking upon its use in a larger project.

A second question to ask is "Does the project involve a lot of 'surge' activity?" For example if a project needs to store and process large quantities of data episodically, such as in support of census data collection, then using a Type 3 Cloud also makes sense.

A third question may relate to the variety of data, such as "Does the project involve combining data from many different data sources in different data formats that need to be processed simultaneously?" It may be that the time required to place all of the disparate data sources into a single, sparsely populated relational database would take longer than placing the same data in an Accumulo format and running map-reduce programs against it. Note that the Data-focused Cloud can be used to analyze both structured and unstructured data, which might be a determining factor for the project. For example, if the disparate data sources are not already in a relational database format, placing the various data into unstructured Type 3 Cloud files in HDFS may be the fastest way to be able to find relationships within and between those data sets, as described in Chapter 9.

A fourth question for the PM to ask is "Do I have a Data-focused Cloud already available for this project?" If the Type 3 Cloud is available and the data is in or can be readily entered into a Data-focused Cloud, then using the existing Data-focused Cloud makes sense. Note that transferring data from legacy databases into a Data-focused Cloud is not instantaneous even when mostly automated. Moreover, the disambiguation of similar data elements might take some time as well.

A fifth question is whether a Hadoop map-reduce programmer and cloud analytic developer are available. These two skills may be available in a single person, or it may require two different people. Either way, it is important to make sure these necessary skills are available, because how map-reduce programs and Data-focused Clouds work is different from traditional legacy databases and algorithms. See Chapter 9 for details.

A sixth question is "Should I use a third-party Data-focused Cloud or build our own?" In most cases, a given project will not have sufficient resources to build its own cloud, but the same question can be asked as to whether a given project should use an in-house Type 3 Cloud if one exists, or use a third-party Type 3 Cloud instead. Note that an in-house cloud also requires the cloud administrative skills necessary to set up, maintain and operate it, which in turn requires personnel with key cloud architecture and operations skills.

A seventh question a PM should ask if using a third-party Data-focused Cloud is whether the service level agreement is sufficient to meet the project objectives and satisfy the risk concerns. See Chapter 8 for details about SLAs.

An eighth question is whether the security provided by the third-party Data-focused Cloud is sufficient for the project's objectives and constraints. (See Chapter 7 for details about cloud security concerns.) According to the Apache Hadoop web page about encryption:

> HDFS implements *transparent, end-to-end* encryption. Once configured, data read from and written to HDFS is *transparently* encrypted and decrypted without requiring changes to user application code. This encryption is also *end-to-end*, which means the data can only be encrypted and decrypted by the client. HDFS never stores or has access to unencrypted data or data encryption keys. This satisfies two typical requirements for encryption: *at-rest encryption* (meaning data on persistent media, such as a disk) as well as *in-transit encryption* (e.g. when data is travelling over the network). (Apache Hadoop Encryption, 2014)

Data-Focused Clouds and the PMBOK® Guide

This final section describes how the Type 3 Cloud might be used by PMs within the project management five process groups and ten knowledge areas as described in the PMBOK® Guide. As with Type 1 and Type 2 Clouds, if the PM's organization already has access to a Data-focused Cloud, then many of the issues associated with arranging a Type 3 Cloud will already have been addressed.

Process Groups:

Initiating Process Group:
During project initiation, the PM needs to determine whether a Type 3 Cloud will be needed to support the project. Will the

project need to store, access, and analyze more than 100 terabytes of data? Is a Type 3 Cloud already available to support this project, either in-house or via a third party? Is there sufficient time to get the data into a Data-focused Cloud? If the use of a Type 3 Cloud is mandated by the organization, the rationale for that use should be documented. The PM should also ensure that if a Type 3 Cloud is selected to support a project, that it is the most appropriate of the three types of clouds available. A succinct description of why a Type 3 Cloud will be used, and how it will be used, is important.

Planning Process Group:

Assuming a Type 3 Cloud has been selected to support the project, and assuming such a cloud is not available in-house, then a third-party Data-focused Cloud vendor needs to be selected during planning. (This assumes that the organization does not already have a standing agreement with a Type 3 Cloud CSP.) If the use of a Type 3 Cloud to support this project is an innovation for the organization, then how the Type 3 Cloud will be used to support the existing or new business model will need to be described.

For example, if a Type 3 Cloud will be used, is the data already in a cloud or does it have to be transferred there? Besides the usual issues of encrypting communications and controlling access to any cloud, there may be additional controls required based on the type of data being stored and analyzed on the Data-focused Cloud.

As usual, risk assessment should include the risk of a data breach, and what to do if the data is temporarily unavailable from the CSP (such as due to a power failure).

Executing Process Group:

If the PM's organization does not already include someone whose job will be to monitor the use of the cloud and the services provided by the CSP, then the PM will need to include someone with sufficient skills and resources to do so on the project team. Other key personnel required are those who can write and run map-reduce programs and personnel that can develop, manage and refine the necessary cloud analytics. In addition, during execution the PM is responsible for the communications among all stakeholders, including the project team and the CSP.

Monitoring and Controlling Process Group:

During project execution, the PM needs to monitor (or have someone monitor) the data stored within the Type 3 Cloud, as well as the performance of the map-reduce programs and/or queries run within that cloud. Other features to monitor are whether the use of the cloud for storage is meeting the expected benefits, or whether there are problems with the efficiency of the system. Making sure the CSP meets the criteria for availability as described in the service level agreement will also be important.

Periodically checking that the data being transmitted or at rest are actually encrypted is also good practice for data in a Type 3 Cloud. In a similar manner, ensure that access to Data-focused Clouds is not retained by former employees when they leave.

Closing Process Group:

If the use of the Type 3 Cloud will continue beyond the end of the project, then the PM needs to ensure the access control is correctly closed out. If the Data-focused Cloud will no longer be used at the end of the project, then the final disposition of the data in that cloud will need to be addressed.

Knowledge Areas:

Stakeholder Management Knowledge Area:

The PM will need to determine which team members and other stakeholders will need access to the Data-focused Cloud. In many cases, only the map-reduce programmer, or those who run canned map-reduce programs, will need access. The outputs of these programs will then be provided to the team members and other stakeholders. Business needs and constraints on who can access both the data stored in the cloud and the processed outputs will determine which stakeholders obtain which types of access. How much data, how recent data, and how soon the processed (via a map-reduce program) data can be obtained will all depend on the needs of each stakeholder. The PM needs to ensure the needs and expectations of the stakeholders through the stakeholder engagement plan, as well as whether those needs and expectations are being met throughout the project.

Communications Knowledge Area:

Communications to stakeholders should include how the Type 3 Cloud will be used to support the project. In addition, the PM needs to plan for how secure communications of data to and from the cloud will be ensured and monitored during the project.

Risk Knowledge Area:

Before selecting a Data-focused Cloud, list and evaluate the risks of using a Type 3 Cloud. Will the recourse for a data breach or for lack of availability be sufficient to the project and its organization? After selecting a cloud, monitor the communications, access control list, and data stored in the Type 3 Cloud for any changes in the risk factors.

Procurement Knowledge Area:

Assuming a third-party cloud will be used to support this project, procurement of a Type 3 Cloud service level agreement (SLA) is a prerequisite to using a Data-focused Cloud.

Cost Knowledge Area:

The use of a Type 3 Cloud will entail costs that must be planned and managed. Besides the amount of data originally ingested into the Data-focused Cloud, there will be substantial temporary storage used in running map-reduce programs, and the outputs from the map-reduce program will usually need to be stored on the Type 3 Cloud as well. The amount of combined initial, interim and output data that will be stored over time will contribute to the overall usage cost over the course of the project. In addition, some clouds ingest continuous streams of data, and age off the oldest data when a set memory limit is exceeded. Setting this limit can manage the costs, but knowing where to set the limit in terms of providing useful data available long enough to analyze is also important. While analytics run against continuous streaming data exist, they often require follow-on in-depth analysis of the originally collected data to support decisions. How long the collected data is stored for follow-on analysis after streaming analytic identified something of interest is another important consideration for a Type 3 Cloud.

Integration Knowledge Area:

The use of a Type 3 Cloud must be integrated into the organization's business model. Will data in legacy relational databases be translated into a format usable by a Data-focused Cloud? Will both structured and unstructured data be sent to the Type 3 Cloud? How will each type of data be used? What will it be used for? Who will have access to the data and why? How will onsite and remote cloud data functions be integrated on this project? How long will the initial, interim, and final output data be stored before being aged off? Who decides how long to keep which types of data?

Scope Knowledge Area:

How will the Type 3 Cloud be used within your business model? Which data will be sent to the Type 3 Cloud? How much data will be stored in the Type 3 Cloud each month? Will both structured and unstructured data be sent to the Type 3 Cloud? How many users will be running queries or map-reduce programs in the Data-focused Cloud? If the scope of using the Type 3 Cloud changes over time, how will that scope creep be managed?

Time Knowledge Area:

When will operations be transitioned to start using the Type 3 Cloud? When will the data be ingested into the Data-focused Cloud (if not already loaded)? How long will it take to complete the disambiguation (if needed)? How long do map-reduce programs run against this data set take? How long are both the input data and the output data retained in the Type 3 Cloud?

Quality Knowledge Area:

What is the time required to complete a given map-reduce program, and does this match the service level agreement (SLA)? How is the quality of service measured according to the SLA? Who will monitor the performance of the Type 3 Cloud provider and how?

Human Resources Knowledge Area:

The key human resource required for Big Data analysis in the Type 3 Cloud is the availability of a person who can write map-reduce programs and someone experienced in developing and refining cloud-based analytics. Map-reduce programmers and cloud analytic developers are in high demand, and the PM may not be able to afford one full-time. However, obtaining even part-time access to a good map-reduce programmer and/or cloud analytic developer is critical to the success of a project using a Type 3 Data-focused Cloud. Without such skills, team members can spend a lot of time retrieving partial or incorrect results from map-reduce programs. Having a good map-reduce programmer on the project, or at least as an advisor to the project, will be essential to the success of the project.

Chapter 7:
Security Issues
and the Cloud

Overview

This chapter describes three broad categories of general cloud security concerns, as well as the solutions available for each. These three categories are physical and geographical security issues, communications security issues, and "Shared Use" security issues.

The second section presents the "seven deadly sins" of common customer cloud security errors and how to fix them.

The third section discusses other cloud security resources, such as online cloud reference architectures from NIST, limited cloud access, penetration testing benefits, FedRAMP authorization, and classified data and the cloud.

The last two sections describe the questions PMs need to ask about cloud security, and how cloud security issues map to the PMBOK® Guide.

General Cloud Security Concerns

Cloud security is a rapidly changing field. Besides the emergence of new threats, or the appearance of legacy cyber threats newly applied to clouds, there are also many recent advances in providing better security to clouds. This chapter presents three general cloud security concerns, their component issues, and recommended security solutions as of the end of 2014. As new security issues and solutions appear, we anticipate that later editions of this book will update this list of issues.

If one is using a Storage Cloud, then authentication and encryption will be essential if you are storing sensitive personnel information or proprietary information. If using a Data-focused Cloud, similar protections should be provided for sensitive data when stored and processed on a Type 3 Cloud.

Type 2 Clouds in particular are usually subject to vulnerabilities within their legacy elements, such as hard drives, operating systems, virtual machines, hypervisors (software that runs between the VMs and the hardware), authentication processes, and software applications. Most legacy threats to these elements are as applicable to cloud environments as they were to legacy enterprise environments. The reason that Type 1 Clouds are less susceptible to many legacy vulnerabilities is that all they do is store data--they do not run programs. Similarly, Type 3 Clouds run specific types of programs rather than legacy applications. Even so, strong authentication and other access control mechanisms are required for users of all three types of clouds, as well as basic protections on underlying operating systems.

In addition to these legacy security threats, there are additional vulnerabilities that are new and unique when using third-party cloud service providers (CPSs):

- You don't control the physical security at the CSP

- You don't necessarily control the geographical location of the data

- You need secure communications to and from the cloud

- You need access control and authentication for your users to the offsite CSP

- Unless you are using a VPC, someone else may be running on the same hardware that your programs run on, which creates multiple potential vulnerabilities

- Since other customers share the same CSP's cloud, brute-force distributed denial of service (DDoS) attacks against another user may affect your access to your co-located cloud assets

New vulnerabilities of virtual environments and even the hypervisors they run on continue to emerge. For example, AWS recently had to reboot parts of EC2 to address a newly discovered vulnerability in the Xen hypervisor. (Burt, 2014)

This chapter will briefly examine three common cloud security vulnerability issues:

- **Physical Security:** How is physical access controlled at the site? Who gets physical access to the site? Where is the site physically located? Where is your data physically located?

- **Communications Security:** You are responsible for securing your communications to and from the CSP's cloud, as well as controlling who in your organization gets remote access to the site.

- **Shared Use:** Unless you are running on your home-built private cloud or a virtual private cloud provided by a CSP, you are vulnerable to co-residency attacks, the possibility that someone can recover your deleted data, and Distributed Denial of Service (DDoS) attacks.

Figure 7.1 summarizes these security issues mapped on top of Figure 2.1:

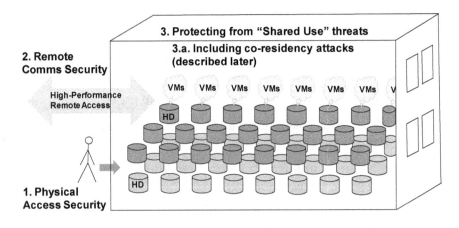

Figure 7.1: Three Primary Third-Party Cloud Security Issues

Physical Security and Geographical Issues and Solutions

Physical security is the responsibility of the cloud owner. If you build your own cloud, you are responsible for physical security. If you use a cloud service provider, the CSP is responsible for physical security. The CSP must ensure that only authorized personnel are allowed into their facilities. Common physical security measures include locks, perimeter controls, guards, CCTV, redundant power, and full-time surveillance of key areas. Furthermore, to protect against an insider threat within the CSP facilities, the movements and actions taken by employees should be monitored to ensure that nothing inappropriate is occurring.

For example, Amazon Web Services (AWS) monitors who is accessing a telecommunications closet. If the person does not have an authorized work order to be in that closet, the security staff are informed. In a similar manner, Google Apps data centers are restricted to an as-needed basis, and the data centers themselves have network and power redundancies. (Schultz and Jain, 2011)

Potential customers should request information on the security procedures and capabilities provided by the CSPs. Moreover, the Service Level Agreement (see Chapter 8) should address what the CSP will provide in terms of compensation in the event that a physical security breach results in financial losses to the customer.

Project Managers and other potential customers can request a site visit to the CSP facilities to examine the physical security provided, but not all CSPs allow site visits. For example, AWS does not allow site visits because part of their security includes not letting others know where their facilities are located. Moreover, since anyone can be a customer, a potential intruder could pose as a customer just to gain information about the CSP's physical and other security procedures.

If the geographical location of your data is of concern, then many CSPs can ensure that the data is replicated only in specific geographical regions. This helps allay concerns on complying with export control restrictions, and concerns that if the data is stored in another country, it might become intercepted in transit by that nation's intelligence services.

Communications Security Issue and Solutions

Communications to and from third-party clouds transit via public communications. Therefore, they are subject to illegal interception for economic or political gain. For example, man-in-the-middle attacks are used by intruders to capture communications in transit. All CSP customers are encouraged to use encrypted communications to and from the CSPs to protect not only each customer, but also all customers that might be sharing the CSP's resources. If your communications security is weak, then an attacker may enter through your communications channel to attack someone else in a shared use area.

One key element of secure communications is stringent access control. Just as the CSP is responsible for the physical access to its facilities, the customer is responsible for ensuring that only authorized personnel are allowed remote access to the site. For example, Google Apps requires two-factor authentication, which in this case is a user password and a token identifier sent to the user's mobile phone. The token is then entered by the user before access is granted. Without access to the user's mobile phone or its communications, a potential intruder would not be able to gain remote access to the CSP. (Schultz and Jain, 2011)

While security threats and protection capabilities continue to evolve, CSPs already have a number of best security practices in place, including but not limited to (Schultz and Jain, 2011; Baxley, 2014):

- Firewalls to help secure the perimeter against unauthorized access

- Intrusion Detection and Prevention Systems (IDS/IPS) to monitor activities within the cloud

- Up-to-date software patches on all servers and VMs

- Multi-factor authentication for any remote access

- Collection and review of system logs and access logs for anomalous activity

- Anti-malware and file-integrity monitoring on the servers

- Regular vulnerability scans, with quick remediation of any vulnerabilities so discovered

- Performance of Red Team penetration testing at least annually or at the time of any significant change in the infrastructure

- Rigorous change control processes, exercise least privilege, documented policies and procedures for password complexity and other host security capabilities. (Least privilege ensures that users do not have unlimited access like many system administrators have. For example, this helps keep an adversary from quickly accessing things they should not if they only compromise a user account.)

In a similar manner, each CSP customer must do their part in ensuring security:

- If the CSP does not provide a firewall to the user's virtual private cloud, the customer must provide one

- The customer should install and manage host-based firewalls and host-based intrusion detection systems (HIDS, anti-malware detection, file intrusion monitoring, log monitoring, and encryption). Anything the customer uses to protect their legacy networks should also be used to protect their VMs and data in the cloud.

- The customer should actively monitor these preceding protections. For example, it does no good to collect log files if the user never looks at them. Alerts that are triggered with no response provide no real protection.

- Since customers manage their own passwords, the customer must generate and enforce password complexity policies, password change frequency, user audits, and other basic security practices.

"Shared Use" Security Issue and Solutions

This section covers three types of cloud-specific vulnerabilities resulting from operating on processors, hypervisors or hard drives shared by other customers: co-residency attacks (including side-channel attacks), Distributed Denial of Service (DDoS) attacks, and recoverable data deletion. Note that while it is a more expensive option, the use of virtual private clouds (VPCs, as described in Chapter 5) precludes the customer from being exposed to all of the shared use security issues (except possibly some brute-force DDoS attack effects) by ensuring that all data and programs run on hardware dedicated to that customer.

Co-Residency and Side-channel Attacks and Solutions

A co-residency attack is one in which another customer with malicious intent is resident on the same processor, hypervisor or hardware on which you are operating. One of the most serious types of co-residency attacks is a side-channel attack. Even though you and the other customer are running on different VMs, some critical information may be gleaned from your transactions via a side-channel attack.

> A side-channel attack is any attack based on information gained from the physical implementation of a system; e.g., timing information, power consumption, electromagnetic leaks or even sound can provide an extra source of information that can be exploited to access or damage the system. (Wikipedia, "Side Channel Attack," 2014)

Note that most of the traditional examples above depend upon the eavesdropper being physically close to the intended target system. In legacy networks, that would mean that the intruder had to be either in your facility or otherwise close enough to detect activity on computer systems. In cloud computing, however, if you and an attacker are using the same hardware, then by definition they are "close enough" to read these minor but detectable signals to capture vital information.

For example, since encryption is a key security element of cloud computing, then an attacker would like to know your encryption key. To detect this information, an attacker sitting on a different VM on the same processor, hypervisor or hardware as you could try and detect the fairly weak signals of your encryption calculations. Even though the hardware environment is electronically noisy, there is sufficient "signal" available to a determined intruder with enough time to capture your encryption keys. (Dark Reading, 2012)

For the attacker to collect this data, he generally needs to either be on the same processor as your VM at the same time that you are, collecting your calculations over time. However, if the attacker has found a way to compromise the hypervisor or even the underlying hardware, then his capabilities and persistence on the cloud is significantly increased. Conversely, the vulnerabilities that allow an attacker to move from the VM to control the hypervisor, or to become embedded in the hardware, are becoming more difficult due to security improvements in this area.

Note that for non-VPC environments, VMs are assigned without an attacker being able to choose which hardware the VM will be placed upon. This makes it much more difficult for an attacker to target a specific user in the cloud. Conversely, any user could be exposed to an attacker who happens to land on the same hypervisor or hardware. An attacker can be pretty sure of finding something on the same hardware, even if it is not the attacker's intent to target your company or data specifically. (Ristenpart et al., 2009) There is also a concern that even with a VPC, if one is rapidly surging new VMs into the VPC, there is a slight chance that the most recently added hardware may have been compromised by an attacker.

While side-channel attacks are a serious threat to cloud computing, there have been advances to preclude them from working within cloud computers. For example, AWS stated that they have solved the side-channel attack problem in EC2. (Private correspondence with Stephen Schmidt, AWS Chief Information Security Officer, October 31, 2011.) Another security solution is the "Home Alone" software that uses side-channel attack software as a defensive tool to make sure that no other users are on the same hypervisor or hardware as you. (Zhang et al., 2011)

Even though co-residency attacks are still a potential problem in many clouds, such attacks are slow, take substantial skill and resources to accomplish, and some luck to find something of interest. It is much easier for an attacker to take advantage of cloud customer errors to gain easier access. These common customer errors are listed later in this chapter.

The Recoverable Data Deletion Security Issue and Solution

Clouds provide another area of concern when others use the same hard drives as you do. The same memory is used by you at one time and someone else at another time. Even though you have marked some of your data as deleted, it may be recoverable by someone else with access to the memory locations where you just erased your data.

This problem is exacerbated by the fact that most cloud storage uses triple redundancy to ensure data is not lost. This is true for Storage Clouds, Utility Clouds and Data-focused Clouds. Even when all three copies are deleted, that still provides three chances that someone else with access to that same memory could attempt to recover your deleted data. (Sun, et al., 2014)

Once again, if your project is using a VPC, this problem is precluded as long as the reserved hardware is not released to others. Another solution to this problem is to ensure that the data is always encrypted at rest. Then, when the data is marked as deleted, someone else trying to recover that data will have to break the encryption to understand any data they might recover. (See also end of chapter 6 on Apache encryption 2014 for built-in encryption capabilities in Hadoop.)

One additional option is to find out whether your CSP has a way to "overwrite" the deleted segments of memory in the event that you are not using encryption. For example, NIST has Guidelines for media sanitation. (Kissel, et al., 2006) Many CSPs do not appear to have special deletion procedures, so users may want to run deletion-assurance software when they delete their data. Even so, the best protection available is to encrypt your data at rest.

Lastly, users can test whether their data has been deleted when using a VPC. Your penetration testing team can attempt to recover data you just deleted as part of your security practices. This can be performed both when evaluating a CSP for use, or periodically during ongoing operations.

Distributed Denial of Service Attacks and Solutions

There are two primary ways in which DDoS attacks can become a substantial threat to a cloud user.

The first is the "ransom" type of attack used by well-organized groups of hackers. For example, the now defunct company Code Spaces was suffering from a DDoS attack against its servers. The hackers had gained access to the CSP's cloud control panel that the company used to communicate with their data. When their ransom demand was not met, the hackers used multiple logins (which they inserted to maintain their attack continuity) and then started deleting the Code Space data, backups, machine configurations, and offsite backups. Code Spaces shut down shortly thereafter. The hacker entry path was probably set up via a spearphishing attack that led to the compromising of administrator credentials. A multifactor-factor authentication scheme could have precluded this problem. "In addition, some level of separation of duties should be enforced by controlling the actions that individual administrators can perform. This could have helped prevent this type of breach." (Greenberg, 2014)

A second type of DDoS threat can also affect performance and availability, but is not likely to lead to such an extreme outcome as the ransom type of attack. In this case, either your organization or someone else's organization housed by the CSP is being targeted by someone wishing to disrupt or deny service to that organization. Even if your organization is not the primary target, anyone operating on the CSP may suffer from the reduced available bandwidth. The good news is that the CSPs tend to have very large bandwidth connections from their Internet Service Providers (ISPs), so that such a brute force DDoS attack would have to be very large in order to significantly reduce the bandwidth available to the CSP's customers. The primary protection mechanism against this type of attack is the size of the CSP's available bandwidth, and the compensations provided by the CSP in the event of reduced availability of their promised services.

In addition, there are software and practices that the CSP can apply when a DDoS attack is detected. DDoS mitigation tools include "...deploying hardware to detect and mitigate attacks locally with automated signaling to divert attack traffic to a cloud-based scrubbing center. The scrubbing center should be able to handle attacks hundreds of gigabits in size, improving the cloud provider's ability to keep your resources up and running." (Lowry, 2014) It is a good idea to find out which DDoS detection and remediation capabilities are available at the CSP.

Common Customer Cloud Security Errors

Even when a CSP provides the level of security sufficient to protect their users in their cloud, often the users themselves do not hold up their end of their security responsibilities. In many cases of detected intruder access, it has been caused by user errors rather than a security failure on the part of the CSP. The following list of seven common cloud user errors (i.e., the seven deadly sins) were generously provided by Dell Cloud Services Security Consultant Barry Baxley (Baxley, 2014):

1. **Failure to administer the firewall at the perimeter of a virtual environment**

    Best practice firewall security includes shutting down all unneeded ports. The more ports that are open, the more chances an intruder has to gain access into or exfiltrate data out of the cloud. If your authorized access to the cloud does not require certain protocols to talk through certain ports, then shut them down. Otherwise, they are open doors waiting to be entered.

    Avoid setting the firewall permission to "from any / to any" or "any-to-any" as this allows the firewall to be wide open to abuse. When a user has found they have been breached, it is often because they had their firewall set to "any-to-any." Configuration audits can not only help ensure the proper settings have been made, but also that they have not been tampered with and modified since originally set.

2. **Failure to monitor perimeter firewall for inbound and outbound attacks**

    Besides setting the firewall parameters to the correct configuration, the user also needs to monitor the traffic to and from their cloud to detect unauthorized entry. For example, if your company does not do business with a foreign company, why is there so much traffic to a foreign IP address? If no one is working late at night, why is there a bandwidth spike at 2 AM?

    Besides monitoring for unauthorized traffic, it is also useful to perform periodic vulnerability scans to ensure that originally correct settings have not been changed by accident or by other unapproved modifications.

3. **Failure to establish and enforce good password policies**

    As mentioned previously, CSPs do not know your password and can't reset a lost password. The user is completely responsible for password management of their access to the cloud. This means, first, that the user has to manage the passwords of all of their authorized users. Since the user is responsible for password management of their users, the user needs to ensure all default passwords are changed.

Second, you need to ensure that all users employ sufficient password complexity, such as the minimum length of the password, the different types of characters (such as using upper and lower case letters, numbers, special characters, and few repeating characters).

Third, the user needs to define an acceptable rate of password changing, which helps protect the cloud access from having the same password in place forever.

Most clouds (and legacy networks) suffer thousands of attacks per day via brute force SSH (remote shell) and brute force RDP (remote desktop protocol) login attacks. These attacks usually start with default usernames (e.g., Admin) and passwords (e.g. Password), but may also be tailored to user names gleaned from open sources and relatively weak passwords. These brute force attacks are the most common forms of attacks at present, partly because they are in expensive and work so often.

Weak passwords will eventually fail, which is why hackers spend so much time trying to get in that way. If the firewall (above) is not monitored to detect and block brute force attacks, that gives the hacker lots of time to find a weak password. In addition, bot-based brute force attacks use a "swarm" mechanism, where if any members are blocked, the others continue the brute force attack. So precluding the use of weak passwords by your users is critical to the security of your access to the cloud.

Note that brute force attacks against cloud users are definitely on the rise. The Alert Logic Cloud Security Report Spring 2014 observed a significant increase in brute force attacks (rising from 30% to 44% of cloud users), and vulnerability scans seeking entry increased from 27% to 44% in the same year. The report noted that while these types of attacks were historically much more common against legacy networks, the rate of brute force attacks and vulnerability scans are now nearly equivalent against cloud-based users. (Alert Logic, 2014)

4. **Failure to install operating system and application patches in a timely fashion**

    Some CSPs provide VMs with the latest patches whenever a VM is spun up for a user. However, the VMs must be shut down periodically to receive the latest patch from the Master VM image. If a customer is using persistent VMs, the reboot cycle needs to be carefully managed. Delayed patch updates in cloud-based VMs can be as much of a problem as delayed patch updates in legacy networks. In a similar manner, the user of an IaaS cloud is always responsible for the applications they run in the cloud. If these applications are not promptly patched, then the VMs running the applications will be as vulnerable as the legacy networks running those unpatched applications. In particular, insecure web applications and APIs (software interfaces) to external software are particularly susceptible to hacking due to their accessibility from the Internet.

5. **Failure to install, run, and patch anti-malware software and host-based firewalls**

    Some CSPs, such as a Desktop as a Service Cloud, provide anti-malware software and host-based firewalls. (See Chapter 5.) Other CSPs provide the hosts and VMs, but all software running on the VMs is the responsibility of the user. As a result, any VMs, especially persistent VMs, need the usual suite of host-based anti-malware software and host-based firewall protections. Just as the hosts on your physical network need protection in case an intruder gets past your firewall, so too do the VM hosts within a cloud.

6. **Failure to actively monitor host-based security controls for sign of compromise**

    Just as legacy network nodes must be monitored for sign of compromise, so should all of the nodes belonging to a user in a cloud. It does little good to have an intrusion detection system warn of a compromise if no one ever checks the alerts and takes appropriate actions. In a similar manner, if the intrusion detection software on

VMs in the cloud sends alerts of compromise, someone better be paying attention to them.

7. **Failure to educate users on the importance of following good security practices**

   Two of the most common successful attack vectors are spearphishing and drive-by downloads. Spearphishing sends the intended victim an e-mail with an infected attachment or link to an infected site. If either is activated, remote access malware is quickly downloaded onto the victim's network. In drive-by downloads, just visiting sometimes even legitimate but recently infected websites can result in malware being downloaded onto a user's network. Your users are your front line of defense. Security-educated users are less likely to fall for spearphishing e-mails or visit infected websites. Also make sure users know how to respond if they believe their node has been infected.

As an example of a PaaS that follows good security practices, Google Apps employs host-based systems that have been custom-built to reduce the attack surface of their installed systems. They also perform internal and external audits of their application code to help identify and resolve vulnerabilities. (Schultz and Jain, 2011)

Other Cloud Security Topics

Useful Security-Related Online Reference Architectures

The NIST website has a number of links for cloud reference architectures and security reference architecture (current as of September 2014):

- Reference Architecture:
  http://www.nist.gov/customcf/get_pdf.cfm?pub_id=909505

- Security Reference Architecture:
  http://collaborate.nist.gov/twiki-cloud-computing/pub/Cloud Computing/ CloudSecurity/NIST_Security_Reference _Architecture_ 2013.05.15_v1.0.pdf

- High Priority Requirements to Further USG Agency Cloud Computing Adoption:
  http://www.nist.gov/itl/cloud/upload/SP_500_293_volumeI-2.pdf

- Useful Information for Cloud Adopters:
  http://www.nist.gov/itl/cloud/upload/SP_500_293_volumeII.pdf

The Cloud Security Alliance (https://cloudsecurityalliance.org/) has additional useful cloud security information.

Limited Access Clouds

As described above, virtual private clouds are a common way to limit security exposure when using shared clouds. The tradeoff is that since your organization is the only user to that cloud, those resources can't be used for any other customer. This makes the provisioning of VPCs a more expensive option for the CSP, and therefore for the customer.

There are two common alternatives to the CSP VPC approach. The first option is to build your own cloud. Note that this can be an expensive proposition. Many of the purported cost savings provided by using large-scale CSPs are lost in this option, and all of the hardware, installation, maintenance, and security of the cloud are the responsibility of the organization that builds it. However, there is a marked increase in the security provided by a home-built private cloud.

A second alternative is Amazon Web Service's "GovCloud" and similar government-only user clouds offered by other CSP vendors. "AWS GovCloud (US) is an isolated AWS Region designed to allow US government agencies and customers to move sensitive workloads into the cloud by addressing their specific regulatory and compliance requirements." **(Amazon Web Service's GovCloud)** If your organization is part of the US government or one of a selected number of contractors, a GovCloud will help provide some of the benefits of increased security (by limiting the customer base) as well as provide many of the financial benefits of using a third-party CSP.

Penetration Testing Benefits

A cloud user can benefit from performing, or having someone else perform, penetration testing of the cloud you are using or considering to use. There should be no reason why a CSP would not allow penetration testing performed on a VPC since no other users would be affected. In a similar manner, a home-built private cloud should have penetration testing performed by its owner.

The types of features to test during a penetration test of a cloud include:

- Are your communications to and from the cloud secure?
- Is the data secure at rest? (I.e., is it encrypted?)
- Can you get access to the underlying hypervisor and/or hardware? Since you as a user shouldn't be able to reach the hardware or even the hypervisor, that would identify a security issue.
- Will a side-channel attack succeed?
- Can you recreate a deleted file?

If any of these penetration tests succeeds, then there are security issues with that cloud that you or the CSP should address.

FedRAMP Authorization

Rather than having each customer independently determine whether a given CSP is able to meet a given set of standards, it would be useful to have an approved, centralized and common method of evaluating the security of a CSP's offering. To provide this common approach, NIST has led and coordinated development of a set of standards that CSPs must meet in order to be authorized for use by government organizations for unclassified and sensitive-but-unclassified (SBU) data storage and processing. This program is called FedRAMP, which stands for the Federal Risk and Authorization Management Program. FedRAMP is now in revision 4, so please check the FedRAMP website (http://cloud.cio.gov/fedramp) for the latest updates.

FedRAMP is a process that describes the minimum requirements for a vendor (CSP) to be compliant when they store unclassified and SBU data. It is a standardized approach to security assessment, authorization and security monitoring for cloud-based products and services. To develop these standards, NIST collaborated with GSA, DHS, DoD, NSA, OMB, the Federal CIO Council, and private industry.

If you work for a federal agency, then any cloud deployments and service models must use FedRAMP-authorized CSPs, or you must build your own to the same standards. As of August 2014, 16 CSPs were fully or provisionally authorized by the FedRAMP process.

Figure 7.2 summarizes the four-step process necessary for a CSP to become authorized under FedRAMP: Initiate request, Document security controls, Perform security testing, and Finalize security assessment. Either a CSP or a federal agency can initiate the assessment process with the FedRAMP Program Management Office (PMO). CSPs must implement the FedRAMP security requirements in their environment and hire a FedRAMP-certified third-party assessment organization (3PAO) to perform an independent assessment to audit the cloud system, and provide a security assessment package for review. (FedRAMP CONOPs, 2012)

Classified Data and the Cloud

One question that often comes up after discussing FedRAMP is whether you can store classified data on a cloud. The answer depends on whether you can build or gain access to a properly secured *government-accredited* private cloud. Note that *no* cloud that allows public shared residence on the same hardware will be approved to store classified information. All users of a cloud that stores classified data must be cleared (and pass other access and usage criteria) to the level appropriate to the data stored and allowed by approved access control mechanisms.

In most cases, building your own classified data cloud is the safest way to ensure that you *might* become accredited by an appropriate government security organization. While a few CSPs are posturing themselves as third-party vendors of classified cloud services, these will require at least the following features (and probably more):

- At a minimum, VPCs will be required

- For US classified information, all the data must remain within the U.S. (at rest and in transit)

- The CSP must provide appropriate, accredited and auditable access control

- Penetration testing must be successfully completed before use and periodically tested during operation

- The CSP must secure an appropriate government security organization's approval for storage and transmission of classified data

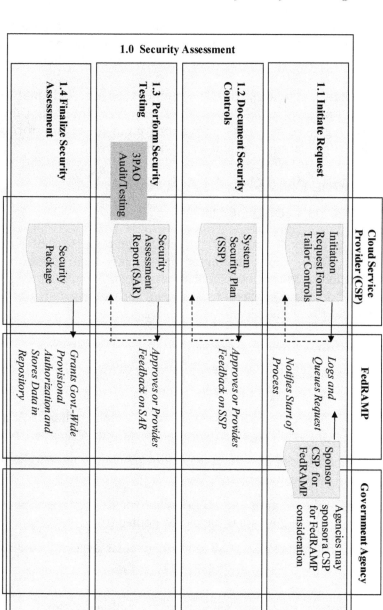

Figure 7.2: FedRAMP's Security Assessment High-Level Overview

In any case, always get a cyber security expert to prepare a risk assessment, and get an appropriate government accreditation approval to store, process and transfer data at that level of classification.

Important caveat: Just following the steps in this chapter *in no way authorizes any user to store or transmit classified data*! Only an authorized government entity can approve the use of and storing of classified information in a cloud or anywhere else.

Questions PMs Should Ask with Respect to Cloud Security

Security is a big concern of companies, government and project managers. This chapter presented the primary security issues and available solutions for cloud security problems. To summarize some of the key points, the following is a set of security-related questions PMs should ask of the CSPs:

- How is physical security provided at the CSP?

- Who gets access to the physical location, and how is that monitored?

- When my data is loaded into the cloud, where will it be physically located (by broad geographical location)?

- Does the CSP provide options for where my data will be physically located?

- When data is replicated, what constraints are applied to where the data is physically copied to?

- How does the CSP plan to protect against brute-force DDoS attacks if they occur?

In addition, PMs need to address the following cloud security questions to members of their own organization:

- Do I want to use a third-party vendor cloud or a home-built cloud?

- Do I want to use a private cloud (home built or a VPC at a CSP), or is the project less concerned about co-residency security issues?

- Does my project require that the data remain in my country?

- How are communications to be secured to and from the cloud?

- How will data at rest in the cloud be encrypted?

- Who will monitor that the secure communications to and from the cloud are and remain secure?

- Who will configure and monitor the organization's firewall logs to ensure best security practices?

- Who will install and upgrade anti-malware software when the user applies them in a cloud?

- Who will monitor the intrusion detection systems and firewall logs to determine whether intrusions are being attempted or have occurred?

- Who will install and monitor the patch upgrades for operating systems and applications used by the project in the cloud?

- Who sets and enforces user password policies?

- Who educates project team members in good cyber security practices?

- Who will perform vulnerability scans and penetration testing, and how often?

If the PM's organization has an ongoing relationship with a CSP, then many of the preceding questions will probably already be addressed by someone within the organization. Such an ongoing relationship can make security issue resolution much easier for PMs.

Cloud Security and the PMBOK® Guide

This section discusses cloud security issues and how they interact with the five process groups and the ten knowledge areas of project management as described in the PMBOK® Guide. To cover the various relevant topics, this section will use a hypothetical project that uses an IaaS for its team members' IT infrastructure, a Data-focused Cloud for its project's Big Data analysis, and a Storage Cloud for the project's archives. As mentioned in previous chapters, if the PM's organization is already familiar with using third-party clouds securely, many of the items listed below may already be addressed.

Process Groups:

Initiating Process Group:

During project initiation, the PM needs to consider the security issues of each type of cloud to be used in support of the project. For example, an IaaS might be used as the IT infrastructure for the project, a Data-focused Cloud might be used for advanced analysis of Big Data, and a Storage Cloud might be used to archive project records. The encryption of data in motion and at rest are applicable to all three types of clouds. In addition, since an IaaS uses VMs as user workstations, a number of the security issues and solutions described above need to be considered for protecting those VMs. Will FedRAMP authorization be required of the cloud vendors being considered? Is an in-house cloud available to support this project? Will a VPC be required? During initiation, the feasibility of the project with respect to its projected use of clouds must be determined.

Planning Process Group:

Assuming a cloud was selected during project initiation, then detailed planning is performed to determine how the project will securely use each type of cloud and monitor its ongoing security requirements. Who on the project or in the project's organization will be responsible for addressing the following security issues?

- Performing penetration testing of the cloud
- Encrypting the communications to and from the cloud
- Encrypting the data at rest
- Providing ongoing monitoring of the encryption security of both data in transit and data at rest
- Taking steps to avoid the common errors or "seven deadly sins" of cloud users
- Creating and enforcing password strength policies

- Training users in how to avoid being easily hacked

Planning is critical to ensure that all of the necessary security functions are performed when using clouds to support your project.

Executing Process Group:

If the PM's organization already has someone whose job will be to monitor the security of the organization's access to the cloud, then the PM can rely on that support to help ensure cloud access security. Conversely, if no one in the organization is providing this security support, then the PM will need to include someone with sufficient skills and resources to do so on the project team. In addition, during execution the PM is responsible for the communications about security among all stakeholders, including the project team and the CSP.

Monitoring and Controlling Process Group:

During project execution, the PM needs to monitor (or have someone monitor) the security features defined during planning. Without constant or frequent monitoring, the project's use of the cloud can be much more quickly compromised. Every time there is a configuration change, vulnerability scans should be performed to ensure that no new vulnerabilities were accidently created. Periodically check that the data being transmitted or at rest are actually encrypted. Similarly, periodic penetration testing is also useful.

Closing Process Group:

If the use of one or more of these three clouds continues beyond the end of the project, then the PM needs to ensure that access control is authorized for those who will need the data from this project. Responsibility for the security of the data in the cloud does not end with the end of the project, but that responsibility will probably transfer to another person. If the data will be removed from or deleted at the CSP, then confirmation of complete deletion is a good security practice to perform at project closing.

Knowledge Areas:

Stakeholder Management Knowledge Area:

The PM will need to determine which team members and other stakeholders will need access to the cloud and to the security management applications run by the project. In most cases, only the security personnel will need access to the user's security applications of the cloud. Other stakeholders may need access to the data and/or applications in the cloud. Business needs and constraints on who can access both the data stored in the cloud and the processed outputs will determine which stakeholders obtain which types of accesses. All team members and other stakeholders accessing data in the cloud need to follow the prescribed access controls and best practices to ensure that the access to the cloud and its data remain secure. The PM needs to ensure the security needs and expectations of the stakeholders through the stakeholder engagement plan, as well as whether those needs and expectations are being met throughout the project.

Communications Knowledge Area:

Communications to and from the cloud need to be secured. In addition, the basis for the secure communications (encryption) and access control (e.g., authentication and strong passwords) need to be properly configured and monitored over the life of the project. While most projects will depend on your organization's IT support for these security functions, the PM should also check with the personnel responsible to ensure that the communications security measures being used are sufficient to protect the content of your project's data.

Risk Knowledge Area:

Security can be expensive. Lack of security can be much more expensive. While nothing is 100% secure, a security risk assessment is essential to determining what level of security assurance is appropriate to the cost of that security and the damage caused by a security breach. Will the recourse for a data breach be sufficient to the project and its organization? Your organization will probably have already performed a security risk assessment for using a CSP, but another, smaller security risk assessment focused on the needs of the PM's project would help determine whether additional (or fewer) precautions need to be taken for this specific project.

Procurement Knowledge Area:

Vulnerability scans, security audits, and penetration testing can be provided by your organization, or they can be procured from third parties. Therefore, penetration testing services may be a procurement action on your project. In addition, the Service Level Agreement (SLA) should spell out the recourse for a data breach caused by lack of security delivery promised by the CSP. Lastly, will FedRAMP authorized CSPs be required, or will a FedRAMP authorization be required when selecting a third-party CSP? If so, either the procurement should be limited to those organizations already authorized by FedRAMP, or if there is sufficient time, one should begin the FedRAMP authorization process.

Cost Knowledge Area:

As described above, providing security when using a cloud for a project will cost money. Will the cost of providing security be provided by your organization's overhead, or will it need to be budgeted as part of your project? Is there a "charge back" from your organization's security providers that will hit your project's funds?

Integration Knowledge Area:

Security should not be a last-minute add-on, but should be part of the integrated project plan. The whole business model for how the project will operate using the cloud needs to include the security measures described in this chapter. In addition, there may be additional or fewer security precautions required for this specific project that may require modification of your organization's standard security plan.

Scope Knowledge Area:

Like the integration knowledge area, the project plan needs to include the scope of use of the cloud in the completion of the project. In addition, the scope of the security concerns and solutions also needs to be included in the project plan and monitored for changes throughout the course of the project.

Time Knowledge Area:

How much lead time is required to ensure that the security functions of the project's use of the cloud are in place? For example, have your team members been trained or recently trained on good cyber security practices, including password strength criteria, or how to avoid social engineering and spearphishing attacks? In addition, monitoring the security status over time is important for both the project and the PM's organization.

Quality Knowledge Area:

Encryption in transit and at rest takes additional time (for both encrypting and decrypting the data). Due to modern encryption methods and faster processors, the additional time required for encryption is not as large as it used to be. To a great degree, the quality of the project's security is defined by the quality provided by the security features described above. For example, following security procedures to avoid the "seven deadly sins" of cloud users will provide substantial security quality. In addition, best practices for encryption include ensuring that the size of the encryption key is sufficiently large, the encryption algorithms strong and well-defined, and that the underlying key management system is not easily compromised. A project's or organization's supporting security personnel should be familiar with, and be able to provide, these encryption features.

Human Resources Knowledge Area:

The project team should include, or be supported by, someone who understands security issues, even if that person is only part time on the project. If the PM's organization has an in-house cloud, or if the organization has standard SOPs with a CSP, then the personnel with the necessary security expertise will probably already be available. Note that the organization's security personnel should at least be able to ensure that the "seven deadly sins" of cloud customer security errors do not occur.

Chapter 8:
Arranging to Use a Cloud

Overview

This chapter briefly describes the wide range of factors to be considered when arranging to use a third-party cloud. The Service Level Agreement (SLA) is critical to ensuring that the CSP provides what is needed for your project, as well as ensuring that it provides sufficient compensations when the SLA conditions are not met by the CSP. It also clearly states what the CSP is *not* responsible for, but that you as a user are responsible for.

In addition, this chapter describes the different types of cloud deployment models—public, private, community and hybrid. It also describes some of the major CSPs active as of mid-2014, including their various pricing schemes, and the factors that contribute to the prices. The final part describes how issues associated with arranging for the use of a third-party cloud map to the PMBOK® Guide.

Using In-House or Third-Party Vendor Clouds

Project Managers may have the opportunity to decide whether their project will use an in-house cloud (if one is available) or a cloud from a third-party vendor. As described in Chapter 7, security issues and risks may encourage the PM to select an in-house cloud belonging to the organization. Given the investment required to build an in-house cloud, it is unlikely that the project itself will own its own cloud. Therefore, the PM should be familiar with what features and services the in-house organization that owns the cloud are able to provide to the project, and the responsibilities of the project team when they use the in-house cloud.

If the PM chooses to use a third-party vendor, a Service Level Agreement will be required. The SLA will be negotiated or selected from a set of previously negotiated SLAs. The PM should be familiar with the factors that should be included in an SLA. Note that as use of clouds becomes more common, organizations may develop long-term standing relationships with CSPs, which will reduce the number of factors PMs will need to consider when using clouds.

The majority of this chapter focuses on the factors that should be covered in an SLA. The next section covers the four cloud deployment models as defined by NIST.

Cloud Deployment Models

The National Institute of Standards and Technology (NIST) defines four types of cloud deployment models: (Mell and Grance, 2011)

- **Public Cloud:** Anyone is allowed to use a public cloud. The physical location of a third-party CSP's cloud is the facility or facilities owned by the CSP. "It may be owned, managed, and operated by a business, academic, or government organization, or some combination of them."

- **Private Cloud:** "The cloud infrastructure is provisioned for exclusive use by a single organization comprising multiple consumers (e.g., business units). It may be owned, managed, and operated by the organization, a third party, or some combination of them, and it may exist on or off premises." Note that a private cloud is not necessarily one that has been built in-house. A CSP can provide a private cloud, or dedicated VPCs that are private within a larger public cloud.

- **Community Cloud:** "The cloud infrastructure is provisioned for exclusive use by a specific community of consumers from organizations that have shared concerns (e.g., mission, security requirements, policy, and compliance considerations). It may be owned, managed, and operated by one or more of the organizations in the community, a third party, or some combination of them, and it may exist on or off premises."

- **Hybrid Cloud:** "The cloud infrastructure is a composition of two or more distinct cloud infrastructures (private, community, or public) that remain unique entities, but are bound together by standardized or proprietary technology that enables data and application portability (e.g., cloud bursting for load balancing between clouds)."

A key point, again, is the fact that the cloud deployment model is not dependent upon the person or organization that builds the cloud. For example, an in-house built cloud does not, by itself, define a specific deployment model such as "private." An in-house built cloud may be kept private, or the owner may choose to open the cloud to a few other organizations, making it a community cloud. Conversely, when someone refers to a private cloud, it is important to determine whether they are referring to an in-house private cloud or a private cloud (or VPC) provided by a CSP. Who built and owns the cloud is an independent consideration from the four deployment models defined above.

Note that for any of these deployment models, whether using a third-party CSP or in-house-built cloud, following best practices for security and efficiency will be essential to the success of any cloud.

Figure 8.1 shows how the cloud types, service models, deployment models and owners together, thereby defining all of the currently existing types of clouds.

| Cloud Type | Service Model | | Deployment Model | | | Owner | |
			Private	Hybrid Community	Public	In-House	3rd Party
Cloud Type 1: Storage Cloud							
Cloud Type 2: Utility Cloud	IaaS	XaaS Variants					
	PaaS	XaaS Variants					
	SaaS	XaaS Variants					
Cloud Type 3: Data-focused Cloud							

Figure 8.1: Cloud Types, Service Models, Deployment Models and Owners

There are:

- Three types of clouds (Storage, Utility, and Data-focused)

- Three types of service models (IaaS, PaaS, and SaaS, with Xaas variants available) for the Type 2 Cloud (only)

- Four types of deployment models (private, community, public, and hybrid, where hybrid is a combination of two or three private, community and public deployment types)

- Two types of owners (in-house and third-party vendor)

Any currently existing cloud can be placed in one or more of the gray boxes in Figure 8.1. (Note that the figure has a third dimension, where the third-party owner is shown as behind the in-house owner in the figure.) Each cloud will have at least one type, may have a service model, will have a deployment model, and will have an owner. Since both in-house and third-party owners often create or offer more than one type of cloud, more than one of the gray boxes may be checked to show the types of cloud offerings available. For example, a hybrid cloud will have elements in more than one deployment model, and will often include both in-house and third-party cloud elements.

Another way to view the cloud type, service models, deployment models, and owners is shown in Figure 8.2. In Figure 8.2, the owner category spans both the in-house and third-party categories as in Figure 8.1, but in this case they are side by side rather than one in front of the other. This allows both cloud providers and cloud users to define in a single template what is needed or available in terms of cloud computing resources. For example, a third-party cloud provider can mark in the appropriate boxes which cloud offerings they are making available to potential customers. (They would also spell out their XaaS variants if any were being offered.) In a similar manner, an organization that has built their own cloud in-house can indicate which combination of cloud types, service models and deployment models they are providing.

Cloud customers of either in-house and/or third-party clouds can indicate which types of clouds their projects will need, which may include a combination of both in-house and third-party cloud resources. Such a template can also be useful for planning future cloud offerings or needs, for both cloud providers and cloud service consumers.

Cloud Type	Service Model		Owner					
			In-House			3rd Party		
			Deployment Model			Deployment Model		
			Private	Hybrid		Private	Hybrid	
				Community	Public		Community	Public
Cloud Type 1: Storage Cloud								
Cloud Type 2: Utility Cloud	IaaS	XaaS Variants						
	PaaS	XaaS Variants						
	SaaS	XaaS Variants						
Cloud Type 3: Data-focused Cloud								

Figure 8.2: Description Template for Cloud Type, Service and Deployment Models and Owners

Sample Cloud Service Providers

The market for third-party cloud computing is rapidly changing. As CSPs vie for market share from cloud users, the pricing structures, SLAs and security offerings are constantly being adapted to attract the largest share of customers. Due to the rapid changes in SLAs and pricing structures, the best way to obtain the most current information is to refer to the online calculators and service offerings provided by each of the CSPs.

Smaller CSPs often provide services within particular niches so that they are not competing against successful economies of scale. Conversely, larger CSPs may provide multiple types of clouds to their customers. For example, most larger CSPs that provide IaaS offerings also provide storage. Many CSPs that provide PaaS or SaaS often provide IaaS as well. This can be useful if your project requires the support of multiple types of clouds.

The following sample CSPs were main players as of mid-2014, but the field continues to change, with new players entering and previous players dropping out. The author makes no endorsements or recommendations on whether or not to use any of these CSPs. The names of the companies are provided simply to give a feel for what some of the CSP market looks like at the time of this writing. Most of the quotes below are from company news releases or officers of the company. All references to FedRAMP authorizations are from FedRAMP (FedRAMP Compliant Cloud Systems, 2014).

Sample Infrastructure as a Service (IaaS) Cloud Service Providers

- **Amazon Web Services:** By far the largest IaaS cloud provider is Amazon Web Services (AWS) with their Elastic Compute Cloud (EC2). Both the AWS East/West US Public Cloud and the AWS Government Community Cloud are FedRAMP-authorized.

- **Rackspace:** Rackspace was formerly called Slicehost. While focusing first on IaaS, it is also shifting effort into PaaS offerings. Its Service Registry is "a tool that enables cloud consumers to orchestrate the process of assigning a workload and having a cloud service respond to that workload automatically... Rackspace has also had a significant role in shaping OpenStack, the Open Source cloud software." (Rackspace Managed Cloud)

- **IBM SmartCloud:** IBM has provided IaaS services, and recently purchased Cloudant to offer database as a service. (IBM Cloud Computing) IBM also purchased SoftLayer for $2B in July 2013. (IBM, July 2014) IBM has also included services to make cloud-based collaboration easier. (IBM Connections Cloud S2) IBM's SmartCloud for Government has provisional FedRAMP authorization.

- **Verizon / Terremark:** Verizon purchased Terremark for $1.4 Billion in 2011. (Higginbotham, 2011) This has increased the significance of both Verizon and Terremark to the CSP community.

- **Google Compute Engine (GCE):** While much more recent than AWS, GCE is aiming to take on AWS in the IaaS market space. Google has been focusing on software-defined networking (SDN) and leveraging its fiber optic networks to compete with AWS. (Google Compute Engine)

- **Savvis:** "Savvis has been in the market for the past two decades... Savvis is also addressing interoperability concerns while making a push for hybrid cloud—having the ability to work with private cloud and move workloads to public cloud when necessary." Savvis recently changed its name to CenturyLink Technology Solutions. (Williams, 2014)

- **ProfitBricks:** ProfitBricks adapted the "InfiniBand protocol, a switched fabric communications link more traditionally used in high-performance computing." The ProfitBricks CEO also claims "we are better able to give customers more for their money by including load balancing, firewalls and redundant networks." (SearchCloudComputing, 2013)

- **NaviSite:** NaviSite is owned by Time Warner Cable. "It provides application services, enterprise hosting, and managed cloud services for outsourcing IT Infrastructure." (Wikipedia, "Navisite," 2015) The focus on managed services provides additional services over a pure cloud offering to "attract mid-market enterprises."

- **CloudSigma:** "[CloudSigma's] solution is really somewhere between managed services and pure cloud computing... Some enterprises will find that more desirable considering they are not giving up total control... CPU performance, RAM size, HD size—they're all sort of independently configurable." (SearchCloudComputing, 2013)

Sample Platform as a Service (PaaS) Cloud Service Providers

Most PaaS-provisioning CSPs provide some programming and runtime environment, such as Ruby, Python, and .NET Framework, and also provide storage and database routines to interact with other services. Many of these PaaS providers also provide IaaS.

- **Google App Engine (GAE)** (code.google.com/appengine)**:** This is the cloud-based development platform provided by Google. See Chapter 7 for the security features provided by GAE.

- **Windows Azure Platform** (azure.microsoft.com)**:** Windows Azure platform provides a range of cloud-based services and has provisional FedRAMP authorization.

- **Salesforce** (www.salesforce.com/)**:** Salesforce's Government Cloud and many of its component offerings (Salesforce1 Platform, Sales Cloud, Service Cloud, Chatter) are FedRAMP-authorized for both PaaS and SaaS. Salesforce bought Heroku (http://www.heroku.com/) in December 2010. By 2013, Heroku's development community had produced "well over 100,000 applications" by Open Source developers.

- **Engine Yard** (www.engineyard.com/)**:** Engine Yard has built Magento on AWS, and provides a "reliable service for ecommerce application."

- **dot Cloud** (www.dotcloud.com/)**:** dot Cloud is in a similar market space as Heroku, and is focusing on developing cloud-native apps.

- **EMC /VMWare's Pivotal Initiative** (www.pivotal.io/)**:** Pivotal is a spinoff from VMWare and EMC, "which combines cloud application development and big data analytics properties into a 1,400-person 'virtual organization' within EMC." Within Pivotal is VMWare's Cloud Foundry PaaS.

- **Cloud Bees** (www.cloudbees.com/): Cloud Bees runs on the Jenkins Continuous Integration solution. While this book was being written, however, Cloud Bees exited the PaaS business and partnered with Pivotal. (Babcock, 2014)

Sample Software as a Service (SaaS) Cloud Service Providers

Most SaaS-provisioning CSPs provide specific software packages for users. With web-based SaaS, no special software is installed locally. Data is also stored remotely, so data does not have to be moved in order to be copied when moving to a new computer.

- **Salesforce:** (See PaaS list above for details.)

- **Google Apps:** Google Applications such as Docs, Groups, GMail and Calendar are provided by Google Apps as SaaS. (Google Apps for Work)

- **Microsoft's Office Web Apps:** Microsoft is offering its software suite as SaaS. (Microsoft Office Online)

- **Thought Works:** Motto: "Powering Great Software Teams." Thought Works is Heroku-based. As an example, Thought Works was used to provide a rapid and secure disaster relief web application. (Thoughtworks)

Factors in Pricing Cloud Services

Cloud pricing strategies are changing very rapidly. When the author first started presenting the cloud seminar in early 2013, the pricing models were relatively simple:

- Memory used per hour or per month
- Number and variety of VMs used
- Bandwidth used to get data into or out of the cloud
- Responsiveness desired to newly requested VMs (faster response costs more)
- User location limits to geographical distribution of the cloud
- Security features included in the CSP's offering

However, by mid-2014, the pricing models of most vendors have become sufficiently complex that most CSPs offers their own online calculators to provide pricing estimates. While the preceding list of factors are still used in the calculators, there are now so many variants available that the use of a pricing calculator is essential to estimating the price to be paid for cloud access.

Storage Clouds have the easiest pricing scheme, in that the price is generally based on how much memory is used per month and sometimes on how much bandwidth is used to get data to or from the cloud. Type 2 Clouds are the most complicated due to the wide range of VMs that can be selected and other price-affecting factors, such as the list above. Data-focused Clouds are a little easier in that the nodes and HDFS are usually provided as part of the access and the memory purchased.

In some cases, there is no bandwidth charge for getting data into a cloud (Storage, Utility, or Data-focused), but there may be a charge for bandwidth used to get data out. For example, in November 2012, AWS EC2 did not include a bandwidth charge for data entered, but for data transfers out, the bandwidth charge per month was:

- Free for the first GB
- 12 cents per GB for up to 10 TB per month
- 9 cents per GB for up to 100 TB per month, and
- 5 cents per GB for up to 350 TB per month.

As of March 2014, AWS EC2 pricing provided a very wide range of options, from a free tier to get started, to low-end VMs as low as 6 cents per hour, to very high-end optimized VMs for as much as $4.60 per hour. (Amazon Web Services Elastic Compute Cloud Pricing) (The high-end VMs are truly screaming fast machines.) On-demand prices are more expensive than one-year or three-year service contracts. Additional categories of service, amount of memory required, options for reserving VMs (such as for use in VPCs), spot options (a lower-cost spot market for available VMs), and cluster computing options are also available. Due to the wide range of options and price interaction considerations, AWS EC2 provides an online monthly price calculator.

In the same timeframe, Rackspace was offering IaaS pricing that started at $30 per month. As usual, customers only paid for what they used. Rackspace runs on OpenStack, an Open Source cloud software infrastructure founded by Rackspace and NASA. Both private and public clouds with all the usual features are available. End users can resource and manage their clouds through an online dashboard. The disadvantages of OpenStack at that time were the fact that security was not built into the infrastructure, and that, due to it being Open Source, there was an observable lack of coordination between the developers of various parts of OpenStack. Work continues to improve OpenStack and to mitigate these problems.

Note that if the PM is choosing to use an SaaS or PaaS variant such as database as a service, desktop as a service, or business process as a service, then the costs of required licenses will also be wrapped into their pricing scheme.

Service Provider Guarantees and Issues

One question a PM needs to ask is whether the compensation is sufficient to cover the costs incurred to the company for the lack of availability.

Just as pricing structures are changing, the Cloud Service Provider guarantees are also changing over time. For example, as of November 2012, AWS EC2 guaranteed 99.95% availability of service within a region over a trailing 365 day period. (AWS divides the world into a number of regions for a variety of purposes, including improved security, as described in the previous chapter.) In the same time period, IBM SmartCloud guaranteed 99.9% availability.

Fast forward to March 2014, and AWS EC2 still offers the 99.5% availability, and more clearly specifies the compensation if the 99.5% availability goal is not reached. If the availability drops below 99.5% but is still above 99%, then customers get a 10% service credit. If the availability drops below 99%, then customers get a 30% service credit.

The PM's risk analysis should not be limited to lack of availability and the compensation thereof. In "10 Security Concerns for Cloud Computing," Michael Gregg succinctly summarized the issues:

> All physical locations face threats such as fire, storms, natural disasters, and loss of power. In case of any of these events, how will the cloud provider respond, and what guarantee of continued services are they promising? As an example, in February 2009, Nokia's Contacts On Ovi servers crashed. The last reliable backup that Nokia could recover was dated

January 23rd, meaning anything synced and stored by users between January 23rd and February 9th was lost completely. (Gregg, 2010)

How will the CSPs address the situation of actual data loss? How will they address data breaches resulting in exposure of sensitive data? What are the compensations, if any, offered by the CSPs in these and similar scenarios, and are they sufficient to address the potential loss? Are insurance companies providing coverage for these types of losses? For example, some companies offer insurance for a minimum cash flow in the event of a power outage at the company. Are similar insurance offerings being made available for loss of cloud computing access?

Some insurance companies are indeed offering insurance for data losses. For example, in April 2013, Lockton Affinity, in partnership with MSPAlliance, announced the availability of a new cloud and managed services insurance. (MSP stands for Managed Services Provider.) Earlier, Cloudinsure also offered underwriting of cloud services. Quoting Tech Target, Reuven Cohen describes cloud insurance as "an approach to risk management in which a promise of financial compensation is made for specific potential failures on the part of a cloud computing service provider. The insurance may be included as part of a service level agreement (SLA) with the provider or it may be purchased separately through a third-party insurance company who works with the provider." (Cohen, 2013)

While the primary recipient is intended to be the CSPs to protect them from catastrophic financial loss, the insurance coverage can be extended to cloud customers—for a price, of course. While cloud insurance may be available from a CSP, it is currently not being offered by the major CSPs. As of April 2013, AWS, Google, Salesforce, Microsoft currently offer only service credits as compensation for lost availability.

Holding Competitions Between Candidate CSPs

Sometimes it is difficult to determine which CSP to choose. It is not unusual for one CSP to provide some features you like, while another has different features you like. In such circumstances, it may be useful to hold a competition between competing candidates to try out the two offerings.

Note that this does not mean that the CSPs are participating in a formal competition. Although a government organization could publish a request for proposal (RFP), it is easier to simply negotiate a short-term contract with two or more candidate CSPs and see how well they meet your organization's needs.

For example, if considering multiple CSPs to provide IaaS resources, set up a small but representative IaaS on two or three CSPs and determine which provides the best service for your organization's needs. This will cost some money for performing the test, but may save your organization substantial funds down the road. Remember that if you want to perform penetration testing as part of your evaluation, make sure that the penetration testing is being run against a VPC, and not against resources shared by other customers.

This type of "fly before you buy" competition is a test drive of each CSP's offerings. This is particularly useful for government organizations that are required to consider at least three vendors before selecting one. In addition, if there is a requirement that the CSP be FedRAMP-authorized, that can also substantially reduce the number of candidate CSPs to consider.

Transitioning from One CSP to Another

A Project Manager may need to transition a project's resources from one CSP to another at the start, during, or at the end of a project. This involves setting up a new SLA with CSP B, and closing out and transferring the data from CSP A. Should the PM have the data from the CSP A sent directly to the receiving CSP B?

No. The primary reason is that unless the PM ensures exactly what was transferred from CSP A to CSP B, there is no guarantee that the data transfer will be complete. For example, if the PM finds that some of the project's data is missing at CSP B, CSP B will simply point the finger at CSP A, claiming that the data wasn't sent. Conversely, CSP A will claim it was sent and that CSP B lost the data.

To preclude this type of finger-pointing problem, the PM should have the data first transferred (probably in chunks) from CSP A back to the organization's network, confirm the contents, and then send the data on to CSP B and confirm its receipt. This avoids the problem of missing data in transit, since the PM confirms receipt from CSP A and receives the confirmation of receipt from CSP B.

Hence, the PM should have the SLA include explicit details for the handling of the project's data in case of the need to transition data, as well as the disposition of the data during project closeout.

Questions PMs Should Ask When Arranging to Use a Cloud

The following is a set of questions that a PM should ask when arranging to use a cloud. Note that if the PM's organization already has a standing relationship with a CSP, then many of these questions will have already been answered. The PM would simply be checking those items that specifically apply to the project.

- Should I select a third-party CSP or build a cloud in house?

- Which cloud deployment model(s) should I use? Should I choose, public, private, community, or hybrid?

- What are the candidate CSPs I should consider that best match my project's needs? Note that your organization may already have an arrangement with a CSP, but the PM will still need to check whether that SLA covers the needs of the project.

- If selecting an IaaS, how many versions of VMs can you choose from?

- If the desired VM configuration is not available, can you build and install your own?

- What is the pricing model of the CSP, and what factors does it consider?

- What magnitude of memory will your project require?

- How much bandwidth is your project expected to use going to or coming from the CSP?

- Does the CSP have bandwidth limits or cost breakpoints for bandwidth usage?

- What type of customer service or technical support is available to a less-technical customer?

- If the CSP does not provide technical assistance, can they recommend another company that specializes in managed cloud services or cloud technical support?

- What are the availability, security and other guarantees provided by the CSP?

- What type of compensation is provided by the CSP when availability does not meet the guarantee?

- If there were negligence in the CSP's physical security that caused a significant data breach, data destruction or denial of service, what compensation would be available to the user? Would these compensations be sufficient to address the potential loss?

- Does the CSP or another party provide insurance for loss of cloud access or data loss?

- How will the CSP address data loss that is the fault of the CSP?

- How soon after a discovered data loss or data breach does the CSP have to inform the customer?

- How will the transition of the data from the CSP be handled at the end of the project or during a transition to another CSP?

Service Level Agreements and the PMBOK® Guide

This section discusses cloud SLA issues and how they interact with the five process groups and the ten knowledge areas of project management as described in the PMBOK® Guide. While arranging for an SLA with a third-party CSP is primarily a Procurement knowledge area, factors of the SLA can affect the other process groups and knowledge areas of a project, especially the risk assessment. If the PM's organization already has a standing relationship with a CSP, then many of these questions will have already been answered.

Process Groups:

Initiating Process Group:
During project initiation, the PM needs to consider whether to use an in-house cloud or to arrange to use a third-party CSP. Even using an in-house cloud will probably involve some shared responsibilities between the in-house cloud owner and the PM. However, the greatest variety of issues and risks are involved in using a third-party cloud. Therefore, arranging the service level agreement (SLA) with the third-party CSP is an important part of project initiation. The SLA needs to clearly define the roles, provisions and responsibilities of the CSP as well as of the PM and the project team. Besides the security issues described in the previous chapter, issues of availability, physical security and pricing must all be considered to determine feasibility as part of project initiation. If your project is for a government organization, then a FedRAMP-authorized CSP will probably be required.

Planning Process Group:
Once a CSP is selected, then detailed planning must be performed to determine how the services guaranteed by the CSP will be monitored by the PM or his/her designee. Roles and plans need to be defined to ensure that project management factors will be adequately monitored. For example:

- Which of the various cloud deployment models (public, private, community or hybrid) will this project use?
- How will the deployment model's function be incorporated into the project's business model?
- Who will ensure that the availability provided over a specified time period match the level of availability promised by the CSP?
- What are the compensations offered by the CSP, and will those compensations cover the financial risks to the project?
- Will the project require support from an insurance policy, either offered by the CSP or from a separate vendor?
- What is the plan for handling a data breach or a data loss event?

- What is the plan to transition data from the current CSP when the project ends, or if the data needs to be transferred to another CSP?

Planning is critical to ensuring that all of the necessary procurement knowledge areas are performed when using third-party clouds to support your project.

Executing Process Group:

If the PM's organization already has someone whose job will be to monitor the performance of the CSP, then the PM can rely on that support to help ensure that SLA guarantees are being met. Conversely, if no one in the organization is providing this support, then the PM will need to include someone to do so on the project team.

Monitoring and Controlling Process Group:

To ensure that the third-party CSP provides the necessary availability, security and other promised services, someone from the project (or organizational designee) needs to monitor the actual performance throughout the course of the project. If the CSP is not living up to its part of the bargain, the planned responses need to be implemented. In an extreme case, the PM may need to transition the project's data and services from one CSP to another during the project. Though a rare event, this may occur on larger-scale project with a longer duration.

Closing Process Group:

When the project ends, the data at the CSP needs some form of disposition. Will it be stored there for a follow-on project? Will it be archived in a Storage Cloud? Will it be retained at the current CSP or transferred to another? How well did the CSP meet the promised services? How will your project's experience with and evaluation of the CSP be documented and used by other projects in future third-party CSP SLAs?

Knowledge Areas:

Stakeholder Management Knowledge Area:

The PM will need to determine the needs of the team members and other stakeholders when selecting or negotiating a Service Level Agreement (SLA) with a CSP. Factors to consider include the types of access, types of VMs, types of applications, required response times, and required bandwidth. These factors will describe stakeholder needs and the type and quality of service required to be provided by the CSP. Business needs and constraints on availability and confidentiality will help determine elements of the SLA. The PM needs to ensure the needs and expectations of the stakeholders through the stakeholder engagement plan, as well as whether those needs and expectations are being met throughout the project.

Communications Knowledge Area:

Communications are essential for all stakeholders in a project. This includes the third-party CSP if one is used to support the project. Who on the project will be authorized to contact the CSP for technical support questions, if provided by the CSP? Who will address shortfalls in the CSP's performance in terms of availability or security? Since a project will probably be using the cloud on a daily or even continuous basis, a good communications plan and its execution are essential to project success.

Risk Knowledge Area:

A risk assessment is essential whenever selecting a third-party CSP. For example, lack of availability to the cloud is likely to translate into some financial loss. Will the promised compensation from the CSP be sufficient to cover that financial loss? If not, will additional insurance be needed to cover the lack of availability, data loss or a security breach? Mitigation plans need to be prepared to help minimize the damage if worst-case events occur. Another risk factor to consider is vendor lock-in. Will the project be able to efficiently and cost-effectively transfer the data from one CSP to another if necessary?

Procurement Knowledge Area:

Arranging to use a third-party CSP is primarily a procurement knowledge area. The service level agreement is the key to defining just what the CSP will be responsible for and what the customer is responsible for. The SLA also defines the costs to use their services, and the factors that define how those costs will vary over time based on a wide range of factors. The SLA defines the compensations provided by the CSP when it does not live up to its part of the SLA. The procurement process should include assessments of the track record for the CSP based on other users' experiences. The procurement process should also consider holding a competition for selecting the CSP as a risk-reduction measure. Lastly, the procurement should also consider the cost and process of transitioning data from the selected CSP to another CSP if necessary.

Cost Knowledge Area:

Due to the rapidly changing field of cloud computing, and the current high levels of competition amongst the various CSPs, the pricing equations for third-party CSPs are also changing rapidly. There are rarely precise terms for each of the various cost factors in using a cloud, leading most cloud vendors to provide a price calculator to help potential customers calculate their costs. The cost factors include memory used per month, number and types of VMs used, bandwidth usage per month (with different costs for sending to or retrieving data from the cloud), virtual private clouds versus shared cloud nodes, user limitations on the geographical distribution of the cloud, and responsiveness required to surge requirements, such as quick-response VM provisioning. There may also be license costs included in the pricing offered by desktop, database, or business process as a service cloud variants.

Integration Knowledge Area:

The use of a third-party CSP needs to be integrated into the project's business processes. What types of cloud services are being used on the project? How will each be incorporated into the project's and organization's business processes? Who is monitoring the quality of service, how and how often? What are the procedures for mitigating lack of service or other cloud-related problems? One or more of the mitigation plan elements described above will be initiated with the intent of returning to normal business operations.

Scope Knowledge Area:

Like the integration knowledge area, the project plan needs to include the scope of use of the cloud in the completion of the project. If the project scope increases, then the use of the CSP's services will probably increase as well. This will result in an increase in cost based on the pricing defined in the SLA. Who on the project or in the PM's organization is authorized to increase or decrease the scope of support provided by the CSP? In addition, the scope of services and their performance as provided by the CSP also need to be included in the project plan and monitored for changes throughout the course of the project.

Time Knowledge Area:

How much lead time is required to ensure that the SLA is negotiated and in place prior to the start of the project? Which of the project's business operations will be transferred to the cloud and when? During the course of project, who is monitoring the performance of the CSP in providing its promised services over time? How much lead time will be required to terminate the SLA in closeout or during transfer to another CSP?

Quality Knowledge Area:

The CSP will guarantee a certain level of availability for a specified time period. That quality of service must be monitored to ensure that the CSP provides either the required availability or the compensation specified in the SLA. In addition, the other responsibilities of the CSPs, such as physical security, might be monitorable, depending on the CSP. Lastly, does the CSP selected need to be authorized by FedRAMP?

Human Resources Knowledge Area:

Most projects will *not* require a person dedicated to negotiating and monitoring the CSP's ongoing achievement of the SLA. Most likely, someone from the PM's organization will have that job. That person or persons must be conversant in SLAs and how to monitor them over time for compliance. If the PM's organization has an in-house cloud, or if the organization has standard SOPs with a CSP, then the personnel with the necessary SLA expertise will probably already be available.

Chapter 9:
Designing Programs for a Data-focused Cloud

Overview

This chapter introduces the concepts behind map-reduce programs and the benefits of Big Data analysis. The reader is only being introduced to the concepts, and not the details of how to write map-reduce programs. However, the chapter does reference online tutorials and the Hadoop "definitive guide," which this author highly recommends.

This chapter describes how cloud computing allows users to analyze unstructured data using parallel processing. It also describes examples of how map-reduce programs have provided insights not previously possible with smaller scale analyses. The chapter also describes the benefits of data cleansing and reducing data redundancies, as well as the questions the PM should ask. The final part describes how Big Data analysis maps to the PMBOK® Guide, and in particular highlights the human resourcing knowledge area to obtain scarce map-reduce programmers.

Terminology

As mentioned in Chapter 6, this book will only be addressing Hadoop Distributed File System (HDFS) and the Hadoop MapReduce programs. We refer the reader to the Open Cloud Consortium website for details about parallel processing programs using Sector.

The map-reduce program environment runs on top of the HDFS file system. Figure 9.1 shows where the Hadoop map-reduce programs fit within the hierarchy from hard drives, through operating system, to file system, to the map-reduce program environment, to the structured data tables.

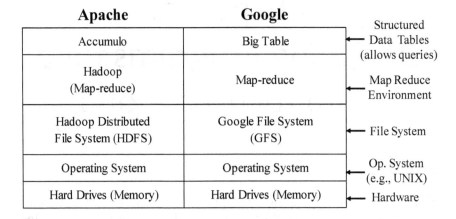

Figure 9.1: Cloud Computing Terminology Comparisons

Figure 9.1 shows the "Hadoop" hierarchy in the left column, while the right column shows the Google hierarchy. Big Tables uses the 5-tuple as described in Chapter 6, while Apache's Accumulo uses the 6-tuple. Either of these tables allows for queries to be run against them, or map-reduce programs can be run against these structured data tables, as described in Chapter 6. The map-reduce program environments in either column rely on the underlying file system, either the Hadoop Distributed File System (HDFS) or the Google File System (GFS). The file system is installed on an operating system, which in turn runs on hardware.

Analyzing Unstructured Data

While Chapter 6 focused on *queries* run against structured data in an Accumulo tablet, this chapter will focus on map-reduce programs that can be run against both structured data and unstructured data, as shown in Figure 9.2. As a reminder, the outputs of map-reduce programs may be stored in legacy applications, such as Excel or Access, or stored in Accumulo, or even stored in files in HDFS.

We will next describe the basic concepts behind map-reduce programs run against both structured and unstructured data, and how unstructured data can be mined in ways previously not feasible to most users.

This book will not teach you how to write a map-reduce program. However, the author highly recommends the book *Hadoop: The Definitive Guide*, 3rd Edition by Tim White and published by O'Reilly. That book will not only walk the reader through how HDFS works, it also provides sample map-reduce programs in Java and links to sample data sources to provide practice.

Note that Tim White's *Hadoop* book is easiest to understand if you already know how to program in Java, but is still informative if you do not. Map-reduce programs can be written in Java, Python, LISP and other languages, but so far the largest library of classes available for Hadoop map-reduce programming are written in Java.

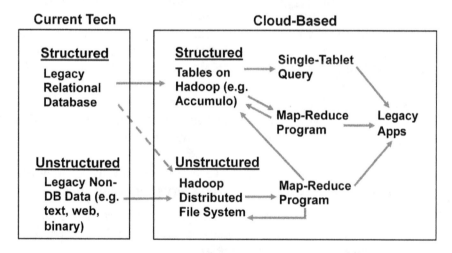

Figure 9.2: Map-Reduce Programs Can Process Both Structured & Unstructured Data

Map-reduce Program Concepts

As noted in Chapter 6, any of the structured data formats (3-tuple, 5-tuple, or 6-tuple) are always of the same width, but can have a very large number of rows. However, because the width is always the same, the list can be split and distributed across many computing nodes. This allows a user to define a single program that can be sent to each processing node and perform exactly the same functions. The results of that program on each node are then combined together at a central location, which completes the program run.

The reason that a map-reduce program has that name is that it is actually a two-part program—a "map" part and a "reduce" part.

The "map" part maps the structured or unstructured data into a "key and value pair." For example, if the unstructured data has the word "degrees" in it, that word could be used as a "key" to select the numerical value next to it as the "value" of the temperature. Thus 56 degrees, 73 degrees, and 89 degrees would be three key-value pairs identified by the map part of the map-reduce program. The map part of the map-reduce program first finds all of these key-value pairs, and places them in an interim format for further calculation.

The "reduce" part takes all of the interim key-value pairs and performs some calculation to produce the desired output. For example, the reduce part of the program may be to identify the maximum temperature, the minimum temperature, or the average temperature (among many possible calculations). The output of the reduce program may be a single value, or it may be a list of things such as the list of all maximum temperatures by day at a specific location.

The examples in the next section will show more details of how map-reduce programs work. The concepts to understand at this point are that map-reduce programs allow users to:

- Readily perform parallel processing by running exactly the same map-reduce program on every processing node

- Run parallel process calculations against *structured* data, such as data stored in many Accumulo tablets distributed across many processing nodes

- Run parallel process calculations against *unstructured* data in files distributed across many processing nodes by identifying one or more keys and values in each file

- Complete the parallel processing by having the "reduce" part of the program perform a calculation on the interim key-value pairs returned by the "map" part of the program

Unlike traditional "high performance computing" parallel processing methods, all of the book-keeping of tracking which data is on which nodes, the balancing of the calculation load among the processing nodes, and the retrieval of the data back to the central location are handled by the combination of the Hadoop map-reduce programming language and the Hadoop Distributed File System (HDFS). All of the parallelizing is handled by the map-reduce program and the underlying HDFS.

In Hadoop, the user is not burdened by these administrative details of parallel processing, but can focus on analyzing the data. As long as the user can identify in the map-reduce program some labels or "keys" in the unstructured data from which to select "values" and form key-value pairs, then Hadoop handles all of the moving around of the copies of the program to the desired processing nodes, and the return of the interim data for the final "reduce" calculations.

Map-reduce Program Examples

This section provides three examples.

1. A map-reduce program run against unstructured census data, returning one value per desired output category

2. A map-reduce program run against unstructured web-page data, returning a list of results per desired output category

3. A map-reduce program run against structured data stored in many Accumulo tablets distributed across many processing nodes.

Example 1: Map-reduce Against Unstructured Census Data

In this first example, the map-reduce program is run against a large number of *unstructured data files* distributed on a large number of processing nodes. These files could be text files, web files, files with numerical data, or binary data. As long as the map-reduce program sent to each processing node can identify a "key," it will look for the corresponding values and produce a set of interim key-value pairs.

In this example, the map-reduce program is attempting to determine the number of households of size 1, of size 2, etc. up to the largest number of people in one household as recorded in the census data files. For the map-reduce program, the key is the text string

"Number of people in a household" and the value is the number of people (a numerical value).

This is an excellent problem for map-reduce to solve, since the census data is probably distributed over many locations, and each person in the household is listed. In this case, we want the key-value pair to be defined such that the key is the number of people in the household, and the value is a count of one for that household with that many people in it. As the map part of the program writes out the interim key-value pairs (Household of size N, quantity 1), Hadoop automatically sorts the results. (See Figure 9.3.) Therefore, the interim data is already sorted by the size of the household. When the reduce phase of the map-reduce program runs, it simply adds up the total number of households of size 1, then the total number of households of size 2, etc. through households of size N. The reduce program is simply adding one for each row in the interim data with the key being a household of size N. The final output is the total number of households of that size across the data set.

In Figure 9.3, the distributed census data is likely to be stored in files created within separate geographical locations. The "map" part of the map-reduce program are all of the light gray boxes on the left of the figure. The program takes the first household and determines the total number of people in that household. That becomes the "key" of the key-value pair. The key is "household of size 3" and the value is "1" since this is the number of households of size 3 in this record. Hadoop automatically sorts the key-value pairs by key, which helps keep the reduce calculations simpler and faster.

On the right of Figure 9.3 is the reduce part of the map-reduce program, shown in dark gray. Since the data is already sorted by key-value pair, the reduce program simply goes through every row in the interim data of key-value pairs, and adds the value (1) for each record of a household of size N. In Figure 9.3, there are 3.5 million households of size 1, while the total number of households of size 2 is 9.6 million, etc. (Note that this is completely fictitious data and does not reflect actual demographic distributions.) The final output of the reduce part of the program is the number of households of each size, 1, 2, through N, where N is the largest number of people in any household in the census data.

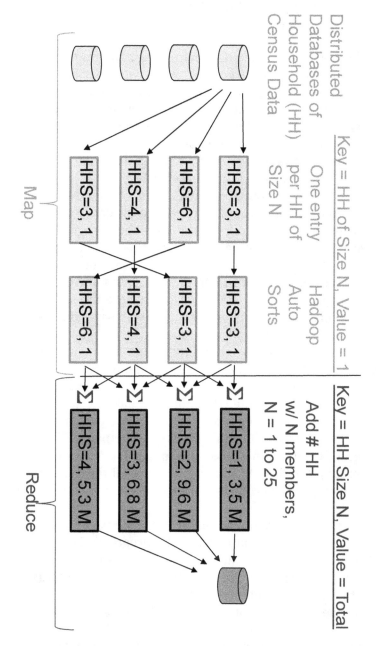

Figure 9.3: Sample Map-reduce to Find Number of Households of Size N

Example 2: Map-reduce Against Unstructured Web-page Data

In this second example, the map-reduce program is run against a large number of *unstructured data files* distributed on a large number of processing nodes. The map-reduce program is attempting to determine how many other web pages point to each web page. Note that it is easy to determine which pages a given web page points *to* based on its embedded hot links. However, each web page does not know what other pages are linking to *it*. There is nothing on a web page that shows that it is the "target" of another web page. I.e., if another web page points to my web page, I have no way of knowing this fact based solely on the data on my web page.

This is a perfect task for a map-reduce program. Each source page is first paired with all of its target pages in the map phase, and then a list of source pages that points to each target page is created in the reduce phase of the program. That is, for each source page, the program creates a key-value pair where the key is the "target" website of every hot link on my source web page, and the value is the URL of my source web page.

The map-reduce program first "maps" each source page to all of its target pages (all of the hot links on that page). The key-value pair stored in the interim storage uses the target page as the key and the source page as the value. Note that to create the key-value pairs, the mapping program goes through each source page and writes out all of its target pages (hot links) as key-value pairs. Then the reduce program creates a list of source pages for each target page, thus generating the desired output—a list of all the pages that point to each web page. See Figure 9.4 for a visual representation of this process.

On the left edge of Figure 9.4, each web page (Doc 1, Doc 2, etc.) is processed by the map part of the program. This is the "source" document of the key-value pair being created. For each target URL in that web page, it creates a key-value pair of the target web page and the source that pointed to that target.

While the map part of the program is providing its interim outputs, it is automatically being sorted by Hadoop. Thus the interim key-value pairs are already sorted by the key, which in this case is the target URL. When the reduce phase of the map-reduce

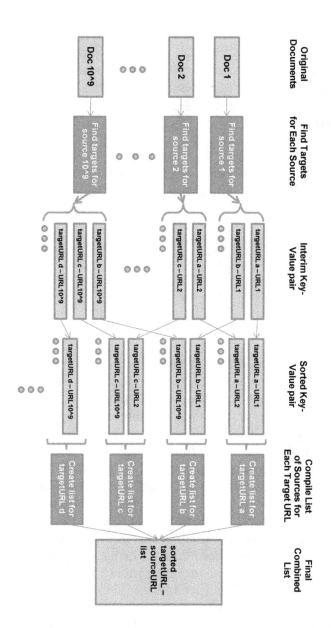

Figure 9.4: Sample Map-reduce to Find All Web Pages that Point to Each Web Page

program begins, it is creating a list of the web pages that point to it, and the process can stop for each target web page when the sorted list is exhausted of that target's key. This makes the reduce program very efficient in that it knows when it has processed all of one target page because the list it is processing is already sorted by Hadoop.

The example in Figure 9.4 is also shown in the following Java pseudo-code:

```
Map (key: sourceURL, value: text) {
        for each (targetURL in text)
                EmitIntermediate (targetURL, sourceURL);
}

Reduce (key: targetURL, value: sourceURL) {
        sourceList[ ] = null;
        for each (u in sourceURL)
                add sourceList[sourceURL];
        Emit (targetURL, sourceList[ ]);
}
```

This is called pseudo-code because there are actually a few more java commands needed to make sure that the map-reduce program knows which Hadoop configuration is being used and other book-keeping functions. But in terms of the "heavy-lifting" of the map-reduce code, all of the essentials are listed in this pseudo-code example. Notice that the output of this second sample map-reduce program is not numerical values, but a list of web page addresses.

Note that map-reduce programs tend conceptually to use a "reversal" step. In the first part, we start with a source page and create key-value pairs from the source to each target. However, in the reduce phase, we are creating a list of the URLs that point to one web page. In the map phase the list of source pages is processed to create the key-value pairs, but in the reduce phase, each target page is processed to identify all its sources. This principle of reversing how the data is processed is a common feature in map-reduce programming. It is not a requirement, but tends to happen frequently.

Example 3: Map-reduce Against Structured Data

In this third example, the map-reduce program is run against an Accumulo table that has tablets stored on different processing nodes. As noted in Chapter 6, the user can use Java programming "calls" that search the Accumulo data more like a traditional database query. However, if there are many Accumulo tablets that need to be examined, running a map-reduce program against many distributed Accumulo tablets simultaneously is faster than running a query-like "call." The reason is that query-like "Java calls" run sequentially, while the map-reduce program runs against the tablets in parallel.

Just as a query can be used to filter on a subset of the data in the table (as shown in Figure 9.5), so too will a map-reduce program search through the data across all the tablets in an Accumulo table to find the desired values. In this case, the "key" is every element in the row except the security and the value, and the "value" is the value at the end of the row. So for the first row, the key is "001, Personal, Name, 31 Apr '12" and the value is "John Smith." (Note that the security element/column is only used as access control to determine whether this user is allowed to see the contents of this row, and does not form part of the key.)

ID	Col. Family	Col. Qualifier	Time	Security	Value
001	Personal	Name	31 Apr '12	PII	*John Smith*
001	Personal	Age	31 Apr '12	PII	35
001	Personal	Height	31 Apr '12	PII	**5' 10"**
001	Address	City	31 Apr '12	PII	Wash DC
001	Address	Street	31 Apr '12	PII	K Street
001	Address	Number	31 Apr '12	PII	810
002	Personal	Name	31 Apr '12	PII	*Peter Parker*
002	Personal	Age	31 Apr '12	PII	28
002	Personal	Height	31 Apr '12	PII	**5' 5"**
002	Address	City	31 Apr '12	PII	New York
003	Personal	Name	31 Apr '12	PII	*Jane Doe*
003	Personal	Age	31 Apr '12	PII	29

⋮ Find the **Names** of those of **Age >25 but <60, and > 5' tall**

Figure 9.5: Sample Query or Map-Reduce Program for an Accumulo Tablet

Our hypothetical "map" program for this example is written to check for the attributes of interest (age and height), and if these are both true, then the value of the "name" attribute is returned. The reduce program returns the list of names that meet the query criteria.

Of course, the map-reduce program can be written to return more than just a list of names. If so desired, many of the attributes can be returned as well. This can be useful if one is planning to send the outputs to a legacy application for further processing.

Note that this preceding example is a trivial for using Accumulo. In reality, there are many more powerful uses for running map-reduce programs in Accumulo, such as determining how many people named "Peter" are in the database, counting them or summarizing by height, age, city, etc. There are many possibilities, which is why cloud computing is so powerful.

Just as the Hadoop map-reduce program pre-sorts the results after the map phase, so do map-reduce programs when producing interim results. In actuality, each Accumulo tablet will not split the row identifiers to land in different tablets. This can be very useful when processing Accumulo tablets in that you know that when seeking all keys associated with a given row ID, all of those data elements will exist in the same tablet. This guarantees efficient map reduce operations because each map process on one processing node accesses all of the row IDs of the same value that are present in the whole data set. It also guarantees that query-like Java calls only need to go to one tablet to access all rows with a specific ID.

Links to Online Map-reduce Tutorials

Many good tutorials are available online for learning map-reduce programming. Just do a search on "map-reduce tutorial." Here are a few of the most popular links as of September 2014:

- Apache Hadoop Map-reduce Tutorial
  https://hadoop.apache.org/docs/r1.2.1/mapred_tutorial.html

- Yahoo Developer Hadoop tutorial
  https://hadoop.apache.org/docs/r1.2.1/mapred_tutorial.html

- Distributed Systems, Map-Reduce
  https://www.cs.rutgers.edu/~pxk/417/notes/content/mapreduce.html

- Cloudera.com Map-reduce Tutorial
  http://www.cloudera.com/content/cloudera-content/cloudera-docs/HadoopTutorial/CDH4/Hadoop-Tutorial.html

- Map-reduce: The Programming Model and Practice
  http://research.google.com/pubs/pub36249.html

- Data-Intensive Text Processing with Map-reduce
  http://www.slideshare.net/inboklee/map-reduce-tutorialslides

- Writing map-reduce in Python
  http://www.michael-noll.com/tutorials/writing-an-hadoop-mapreduce-program-in-python/

- Map-reduce: How to
  http://pages.cs.wisc.edu/~gibson/mapReduceTutorial.html

Benefits of Map-reduce Programs

One of the greatest benefits of map-reduce programs is that they allow the user to find correlations and relationship among *unstructured* data. This means that the user can store a set of dramatically different data files, each with their own format and collected from different sources, and still be able to quickly and easily perform parallel processing of that data to obtain interesting results. This is a significant advance in computing capabilities because the data does not first have to be *structured* in order to be effectively analyzed. No longer does one have to place all of the relevant data into a structured relational database before being able to adequately analyze the data.

Another significant benefit is that the map-reduce program and underlying distributed file structure handle all of the bookkeeping necessary to efficiently perform parallel processing. This has allowed parallel processing to emerge from the realm of specialized high performance computers and programmers into a relatively simple set of map-reduce programming instructions. Map-reduce programming has facilitated the advance of parallel programming for the masses.

Map-reduce programs are relatively small and simple compared to many legacy parallel processing codes. This allows the map-reduce program to be readily distributed to the processing nodes where the data is located. Moreover, the map-reduce programs automatically sort the interim and final data sets. This automatic sorting makes calculation easier due to both the programmer and the program knowing that all data related to that key-value pair are located together. For example, one knows that one can end the processing of one of the elements in the reduce step output as soon as the next variable's data begins. That's because the data is automatically sorted, so all processing on a single variable is completed when the program reaches the end of that element in a sorted list.

Due to the parallel processing capabilities of map-reduce programs, the sizes of the data sets that can be analyzed are dramatically larger than previously possible. Being able to process many petabytes of data in parallel provides much greater capabilities than the legacy relational databases, which are traditionally limited to less than a petabyte and often only hundreds of terabytes or less.

Many individuals and organizations have been leveraging these new capabilities. The ability to find relationships not previously identified has become available to a wide range of businesses and medical organizations. As described briefly in Chapter 6, Big Data was used to calculate bakery sales forecasts based on weather forecasts. In wet, cold weather, cake was purchased more often, while in hot weather grilled sandwiches were more popular. As described in one of IBM's online case studies:

> With the help of IBM® SPSS® Statistics, meteolytix GmbH developed precise, accurate sales forecast models based on weather data, historical sales and information about other contributing factors. The result is a self-learning automatic closed loop statistical model which increases revenue and lowers costs by minimizing over- and under-production. (IBM, "Meteolytix," 2011)

For an example of using Big Data in healthcare, Wellpoint Inc. applied Big Data to their unstructured data to assist in their treatment pre-approval process. For a large number of their cases, the new approach provided responses to treatment requests in seconds, compared to the 72 hours for urgent pre-authorization or three to five days for elective procedures. "The system was put into live healthcare production environment in December 2012. It currently handles 70 percent of outpatient requests across WellPoint's mid-west affiliates. Today, 15,835 healthcare provider offices use the system." (IBM, "Watson," 2014)

The IBM website has a wide range of interesting and wide-ranging Big Data case studies. (IBM Case Studies)

Examples of the ability to find useful patterns in Big Data are becoming increasingly common. If you are a Facebook user and tag one of your friend's posted photographs with their name, then whenever that face appears on Facebook on a different post, the new photos will be automatically tagged with their name. The tagging accuracy isn't perfect, so sometimes likely tags are suggested rather than placed automatically. Whether or not tagging is automated is also a preference setting. According to the Facebook website:

> We currently use facial recognition software that uses an algorithm to calculate a unique number ("template") based on someone's facial features, like the distance between the eyes, nose and ears. This template is based on your profile pictures and photos you've been tagged in on Facebook. We use these templates to help you tag photos by suggesting tags of your friends. If we can't suggest a name automatically, we'll group similar photos together so you can tag them quickly. (Facebook)

Besides being useful, Big Data capabilities also have a number of implications for personal privacy. One classic Big Data example comes from the 2012 Charles Duhigg article titled "How Companies Learn Your Secrets." (Duhigg, 2012) Among other examples, he included the story of how Target was able to determine that a 16-year-old girl was pregnant before her family knew, and sent her pregnancy-related coupons. Why would Target be interested in such personal data? Because most people shop out of habit, shopping at the same stores, buying the same types of things, except when there are major life-changing events. Life-changing events include moves, marriages, divorces, deaths and having children. If Target could predict when someone was pregnant, they could leverage the narrow window of this life-changing event and potentially altering the customer's shopping habits. The article claims that Target, by tracking about 16 or so individual shopping factors, was able to determine when their shoppers were pregnant, and would target them with appropriate coupons.

Of course, most people find that degree of knowledge about shoppers is rather disconcerting, and according to the article, Target changed how they sent their coupons to make their degree of knowledge about their shoppers less obvious. Another article published in 2014 by Gregory Piatetsky questioned whether the story about the girl was actually valid, but the article did confirm that Target was researching the topic of predicting pregnancy from customer purchasing pattern data. (Piatetsky, 2014)

Consumer privacy concerns continue to be raised because the use of the data is often unregulated. While user data can be anonymized when collected, there are now techniques that can re-identify persons from the remaining data. This capability bypasses the intent of anonymization, but is currently still legal. There are also ways to fingerprint your browser even if you select "browse anonymously." (Nikiforakis and Acar, 2014)

In spite of these issues, map-reduce programs applied to Big Data have created huge opportunities to leverage unstructured data via widely available parallel processing capabilities to identify useful relationships not previously identified. It has also taken previously inefficient repetitive computing processes and made them efficient.

For example, NASA's Emily Law presented a paper titled "Imagery Processing on the Cloud," describing how NASA improved access to images in its Lunar Mapping and Modeling Portal (LMMP) for users with memory-constrained desktops and mobile devices. NASA used the cloud to create smaller but comprehensive image tiles from much larger image mosaics that were each several gigapixels in resolution and gigabytes in size. Many smart digital platforms such as laptop, desktops and mobile devices are resource constrained and do not have the processing power to render large size images. When images are not stored locally, they have to be transferred from remote machines and are highly dependent on network bandwidth. To eliminate these limitations, LMMP used the cloud to execute an *image tiling* process that breaks up large images into smaller parts. The parts were then merged and resized until the final image was reasonably sized, but encompassed the scope of the entire original image. (See Figure 9.6.) While the process of tiling is computationally intensive, it is also incredibly parallelizable, and cloud computing enabled NASA to distribute the processing across multiple machines. This significantly improved performance of LMMP's data access and visualization. (Law, 2012)

Note that to process imagery, one needs some imagery software that identifies something of interest in the binary data provided. The binary data is stored in the "value" section of the key-value pair, and the map and reduce parts of the program can use imagery algorithms that can make sense of the binary imagery values.

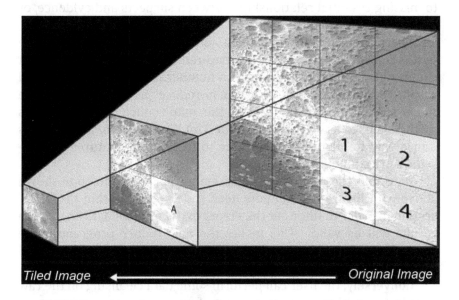

Figure 9.6: Sample Imagery Reduction Process Using Cloud Computing

The Value of Data Cleansing

One of the foundational tenants of Big Data analysis is that it doesn't matter if the data is "dirty" or full of errors. The assumption is that there will be enough "clean" data in the data to swamp the effects of the errors. This assumption does appear to be valid in many applications, where the desired output is intended to define fairly broad relationships or findings. However, when the desired outputs are very specific, then the effects of errors on the smaller data set of interest may have a significant effect on the outcomes.

If your project's use of Big Data depends on finding relationships among relatively small numbers of data items found within a very large volume of data, then the errors in the large volume might have an effect on your findings. For example, when prosecuting a criminal case, errors in the data can lead to false identification of relationships between suspects and disparate sources of evidence. For a Law Enforcement organization, finding these relationships and making sure they are accurate are required to successfully identify the perpetrator and lead to a conviction. Errors in the data can lead to missing essential relationships between suspects and evidence, or contribute to misidentification.

There are usually two ways to address errors in Big Data. The first is to run a relatively simple map-reduce program and see what comes out. If the results indicate a number of errors in the desired results, then modify the simple map-reduce program to eliminate those specific errors and rerun the map-reduce program. This method is used as an example in the Tim White *Hadoop* book, and is a nice way to introduce the novice to the various features of map-reduce programming.

Note that the relatively simple map-reduce pseudo-code shown above with Figure 9.4 will now need code at least within the "map" section in order to filter out the errors in the original data so that the results will be valid. This makes the map-reduce programs more complicated, and requires multiple iterations of modifying and running the map-reduce program to obtain the desired answer.

Conversely, the user can perform some data cleansing on the raw data to try to eliminate the sources of error prior to running more specific map-reduce programs. This will allow the subsequent map-reduce programs to be much simpler, and will eliminate many potential data errors before they can create problems. However, this means that some work must be done up front on the raw data before more specific map-reduce programs are run against the data. Note that map-reduce programs can also be used to facilitate the data cleansing process, which can be helpful given the size and variety of data involved. The output of those map-reduce programs would be another copy of the original data, minus the errors addressed by those programs. For example, if one has data in an Accumulo tablet where the time stamp shows the data was collected in the future, those rows could removed. Alternatively, if the time correction factor is known, then the data could be output with the corrected date.

In summary, the two approaches to error detection and elimination in big data sets are:

1. Run map-reduce programs specifically designed to detect and correct errors in the original data set and use these results to clean the original data set. All subsequent map-reduce programs can be simpler because most of the errors in the data set have already been eliminated

2. Leave the errors in the data set but be aware that every map-reduce program created and run against this data set will need error detection and correction code embedded within it.

Both approaches have their advantages and disadvantages. The deciding factor will generally be how much time and money it will take your project to cleanse the data once and for all, or how much time and money it will take to repeatedly add error-catching code in all of your map-reduce programs. Again, a key factor is whether the results desired from the map-reduce program are fairly broad or very specific. If very specific, then cleaning the data once and for all is preferred. If the desired results are fairly broad, then up-front data cleansing is less necessary.

One particularly troublesome source of data errors is duplicate data. If two data sources provide data on the same person, for example, but the user does not know it is the same person, and this happens frequently, there can be a substantial amount of erroneous counts of the same people multiple times, thereby providing invalid results. De-duplication of data, and in particular identifying whether the same person or item is being referred to by different data sources, is a common problem in dirty data.

Questions PMs Should Ask About Map-Reduce Programs

The most commonly asked question the author has heard from project managers is "Do I need to know how to write a map-reduce program to manage a project that uses cloud computing and Big Data?" The answer is no. A Project Manager often has programmers working for him or her, and map-reduce programming is another type of programming skill. The PM does not need to know how to write a map-reduce program.

That being said, it is very useful for a project manager to know the basic concepts behind map-reduce programming and how to design such a program. For example, knowing the following will be useful for PMs in terms of knowing how to correctly apply map-reduce programs to their project:

- That map-reduce programs can be applied to both structured and unstructured data

- That unstructured data can include many types of data, including text, numbers, URLs, or even binary data (such as imagery)

- That some key-value pair must be identified in unstructured data for the map-reduce program to work

- That the outputs of map-reduce programs can be values, lists, or subsets of the original data with lots of attributes attached to retrieved data items

- That the map-reduce program tends to perform a reversal of the original data into the key-value pair and places these values in interim memory that is automatically sorted

- That the reduce program takes these interim key-value pairs and performs a set of calculations on them to produce the final results

- That error detection and resolution might be needed depending on the specificity of the desired outputs, and

- That if needed, error detection or correction can be done once at the beginning before running a lot of map-reduce programs, or can be performed within each map-reduce program

Being aware of the concepts and tradeoffs will help a PM manage the map-reduce programmers and help provide additional quality assurance. For example, prior to knowing how to run map-reduce programs, the author had a map-reduce programmer provide some sample outputs from a data set. By performing some quick sanity checks on the outputs to see whether they made sense, the author was able to identify what had most probably gone wrong in the program. This input helped the map-reduce programmer figure out how to fix his program.

"How familiar with the original data should the PM be?" It is very useful for PMs to make themselves familiar with the data types available, and sample the data for quality and types of possible errors. Note that relatively small map-reduce programs can also be used to efficiently perform this sampling.

In a similar manner, the PM should ask "How clean does the original data have to be to support the types of findings that are desired from the data outputs?" If the desired outputs of the map-reduce program are fairly broad, then many of the most common types of errors in the data will not significantly affect the findings. If the desired outcomes are very specific and detailed, then there will be the need for either data cleansing before running map-reduce programs, or having error-detection and correction in each map-reduce program.

Lastly, but most importantly, it is essential for a PM to obtain a good map-reduce programmer for a project that will use map-reduce programs. Like any programming field, there are good programmers and bad programmers. Every effort should be made to obtain at least one top-notch map-reduce programmer on the project, or at least have access to that programmer for advice. Otherwise, the project could waste a lot of time analyzing misrepresentative data.

Map-reduce Programs and the PMBOK® Guide

This section discusses map-reduce programs and how they interact with the five process groups and the ten knowledge areas of project management as described in the PMBOK® Guide.

Process Groups:

Initiating Process Group:

The most important element of initiation is to determine whether map-reduce programming will be used to support this project. If so, this leads to the need to obtain at least one good map-reduce programmer. (See human resources knowledge area below.) It is also important to determine how map-reduce programming will be used to achieve the project's objectives.

Planning Process Group:

If map-reduce programming will be used on this project, how will map-reduce programming be incorporated into the project's plan and business model? Who will design the desired outputs? Who will run the programs? Who will perform quality checks on the outputs? Who will further analyze the outputs of the map-reduce program? Will the project need to perform some data cleansing at the start of the project, or just add error detection and correction code to every map-reduce program developed for the project? How much data and what types of data will be needed to support this project? Does the data include structured and unstructured data? If so, how will each contribute to the achievement of the project's objectives?

Executing Process Group:

When building the team, ensure that sufficient personnel with map-reduce programming skills and data analysis skills are available to achieve the Big Data analysis goals within the time and budget available. Perform quality assurance on the input data, output data, and analytic results. Perform a simple sanity check on the outputs to make sure they make sense.

Monitoring and Controlling Process Group:

During project execution, the PM needs to monitor the quality and findings of the map-reduce programs. Always perform sanity checks to make sure the outputs of map-reduce programs actually make sense. Check for new types of data errors that may appear over time that were not obvious at the start of the project. Periodically have an external map-reduce expert review the programs and the findings to make sure something important was not missed. Lastly, ensure that the promised calculation performance of the Type 3 Cloud is being provided when the map-reduce programs are run.

Closing Process Group:

At the end of the project, some of the map-reduce programs will have been found to be more beneficial than others. Make sure that the most useful map-reduce programs are stored and documented for later use by other projects. Collecting a list of lessons learned about the types of original data errors and how they were resolved would also be useful. As with Storage and Utility Clouds, ensure that the final disposition of the data in the cloud is executed before the end of the project.

Knowledge Areas:

Stakeholder Management Knowledge Area:

The PM will need to determine which team members and other stakeholders will need to run map-reduce programs, or view the outputs of map-reduce programs. In most cases, only the map-reduce programmer, or those who run canned map-reduce programs, will need to run map-reduce programs. The outputs of these programs will then be provided to the team members and other stakeholders. Business needs and constraints on who can access both the data stored in the cloud and the processed outputs will determine which stakeholders obtain which types of accesses. How much data, how recent data, and how soon the processed (via a map-reduce program) data can be obtained will all depend on the needs of each stakeholder. The PM needs to ensure the needs and expectations of the stakeholders through the stakeholder engagement plan, and ensure that those expectations are being met throughout the project.

Communications Knowledge Area:

Since map-reduce programming is a fairly new and specialized area, the communications plan will be essential to helping prepare stakeholder expectations. Some stakeholders may be more skeptical of Big Data analysis, while others might believe in it too much. The communications plan should clearly describe just what this project plans to accomplish using map-reduce programming. It might also be useful to describe what will *not* be accomplished, in order to better manage expectations.

Risk Knowledge Area:

The primary risks of Big Data analysis are data quality and misleading map-reduce results. The adage "Garbage-in, garbage-out" definitely applies to Big Data as in any other field. Make sure that the risks associated with the data quality with respect to the desired outputs are well understood and that a mitigation plan is in place. Also ensure that quality assurance checks on the findings from the map-reduce programs are vetted to ensure that the results actually mean what they appear to mean. Remember that Big Data finds correlations. Correlation does not prove cause and effect relationships. Correlation results can be useful, but the leap to a cause-and-effect relationship may be short and reasonable or long and risky. Another risk is related to the availability of access to the Data-focused Cloud when needed. The loss of connectivity to the Type 3 Cloud can significantly affect project timelines that rely on extensive and timely running of map-reduce programs.

Procurement Knowledge Area:

If the map-reduce programming support will be provided to the project via a subcontract, then all of the concerns described under the human resources knowledge area above applies here as well. If a Type 3 Cloud is not readily available to the project, then procurement of the Type 3 Cloud needs to address the points in Chapter 6 under procurement.

Cost Knowledge Area:

Depending on the size of the data set available and the number of processing nodes available at the Type 3 Cloud, each map-reduce program run will incur a cost. The more often the map-reduce program executes correctly the first time, the less the cost to perform the overall analysis. The overall cost of the project can be reduced by having good map-reduce programmers, and by performing checks on small samples of the data to identify the different types of errors possible.

Integration Knowledge Area:

The PM needs to determine how the map-reduce programming will be integrated into the project's plan and business model. Other integration issues include where the original data is coming from, how often, and how the outputs of the map-reduce programs will be further processed by legacy applications (if any). Other integration factors include the owner of the cloud upon which the map-reduce programs will be run, and the providers from the data or data feeds, if not created solely by the project.

Scope Knowledge Area:

The project scope will determine the scope of the map-reduce programs used in support of the project. It is also important to ensure that the scope is managed so that the types, size and quality of the map-reduce program outputs are not adversely affected. The number of map-reduce programs that are run and the time and memory required to run each program will define the scope of many of the costs and risks of map-reduce programming.

Time Knowledge Area:

Depending on how much data is being processed, map-reduce programs can take many hours to run. Many projects run map-reduce programs overnight so that their outputs will be available to analysts the next morning. Managing the scheduling of large map-reduce programs within a larger set of projects must be considered for meeting project deadlines. In addition, running small map-reduce jobs on single or a few nodes of sample data is an efficient and timely way to identify errors and the assurance that achievement of the desired outcomes is possible.

Quality Knowledge Area:

As described above, always perform a quality check of both the data being analyzed and the output of the map-reduce programs. Make sure that the outputs are credible given the possible types of data errors and the results of smaller sample runs. Also ensure that the quality of service promised by the Data-focused Cloud CSP is being provided.

Human Resources Knowledge Area:

This is the most important knowledge area for a PM to accomplish with respect to a project that plans to use map-reduce programming. Having a good map-reduce programmer on the project, or at least as an advisor to the project, will be essential to the success of the project.

Chapter 10: Summary

This book has covered a lot of material and many new concepts and mental models. This last chapter will summarize many of the key points presented in this book, and help the reader retain the main points. It would be useful to the reader to recall, refer back to, or even draw from memory the key figures from the book that are described by the text below.

Types of Clouds

There are three different types of clouds (Storage Clouds, Utility Clouds, and Data-focused Clouds), each with their own capabilities and limitations that PMs need to be aware of. Storage Clouds have lots of memory, but no ability to support calculations or run applications. Utility Clouds provide compute power as a service by offering IT infrastructure, environments, or software on demand. Utility Clouds do not, however, provide the parallel processing capabilities of a Data-focused Cloud. Data-focused Clouds provide the ability to perform Big Data analysis by making parallel processing available to just about anyone, as well as the ability to analyze both structured and unstructured data. Data-focused Clouds do not, however, allow you to replicate your traditional office environment or run legacy enterprise applications.

Planning and monitoring project IT costs are somewhat different when using clouds. All three types of clouds follow the pay-as-you-go model. You only pay for the memory you use in a Storage Cloud, you pay only for the virtual machines (VMs) you use in a Utility Cloud, and you pay only for the time, memory and processing nodes you use in a Data-focused Cloud. This can significantly reduce the cost of ownership for an organization in terms of not owning all their own IT infrastructure and simply leasing what is needed when it is needed from Cloud Service Providers (CSPs). This is a particularly appealing option for start-ups and for organizations with periodic IT surge requirements.

The large third-party CSPs can offer these services and still make a profit because of the Economies of Scale. By using commodity hardware and automating most of their installation and maintenance processes, the larger CSPs can provide a wide range of services in one or more types of cloud at reasonable prices and still make a good profit. Organizations can also choose to build their own clouds (and often do), but the owner of the cloud is now responsible for all of the installation and maintenance, which must be covered via in-house resources. In most cases, building one's own cloud is unlikely to be as cost-effective as using a third-party CSP's cloud, but it may be more secure. Depending on organizational policies, PMs may have a choice in whether in-house or third-party clouds can be used in support of their project.

Type 2 Cloud Service Models

The Type 2 Cloud (Utility Cloud) is further subdivided into three primary types of Service Models: Infrastructure as a Service (IaaS), Platform as a Service (PaaS), and Software as a Service (SaaS). IaaS is what one would choose to attempt to replicate your enterprise office capabilities within the cloud. Those IT resources would be accessed by the organization via remote communications to the cloud. PaaS provides an environment, like an applications development environment, to users who would like the capabilities of that environment without having to purchase all of the software and support structure themselves. SaaS provides users access to a specific software package that can be accessible to a group of users anywhere in the world via Internet access.

These three primary service models (IaaS, PaaS, and SaaS) also have a number of variants, such as Desktop as a Service (DaaS), Database as a Service (DBaaS), or Business Process as a Service (BPaaS). There are many XaaS variants, and more are emerging as CSPs attempt to find niches to meet growing customer needs. PMs therefore have a range of options available to them in terms of the type of Utility Clouds available to support their project.

An additional advantage of Utility Clouds is the ability to provide centralized patch management. Since Utility Clouds use a lot of VMs, the CSP only needs to patch the operating system or application of the master copy. All instances of the master VM created to populate an IaaS (for example) will be created based on the most up-to-date version of operating system and application. This reduces the vulnerability of the IT infrastructure being leased by the customer, and significantly reduces the maintenance costs since patching does not have to be performed on every physical machine. Only the VMs that are spun up on demand need to be patched, and they are patched automatically by being copied from the master copy.

Cloud Deployment Models

All three types of clouds can be deployed in any of the following four models: public, community, private, and hybrid. Public clouds are available to anyone (who can pay for the access); community clouds are available to a set of registered organizations, such as a community of interest; and a private cloud is usually reserved for users from a single organization. A hybrid cloud is some combination of a private, community, or public cloud. Note that a private cloud may have been built by a third-party CSP, or may have been built in-house by an organization for its own exclusive use. A cloud is private based on its access, not based on who built it. The PM may or may not have a choice as to which type of cloud deployment model will be applicable or available to their project based on organizational policies.

Security in the Cloud

Most of the security issues resulting from moving to the cloud are related to a) the cloud being remote from your organization's physical location, and b) the fact that for public, community or hybrid clouds, a user is often sharing their portion of the cloud with other users.

The issue of the cloud being remote from your organization has several inherent security issues, such as who is providing physical security and how, who has authorized access and why, where is your data physically located, and whether your access to your data in the cloud will be available when you need it. Some solutions to these issues are provided by CSPs that: have good physical security and access control, offer regional limitations on the location that your data can be stored, and offer some guarantees on availability. The project's security requirements will help the PM select which of the available solution options can provide sufficient security.

The issue of "shared use" means that in a general public or even some community clouds and hybrid clouds, others on the same hypervisor or hardware as you might be able to "snoop" on your transactions (such as trying to determine your encryption keys) or attempt to reconstruct from memory data you deleted. Using a virtual private cloud (VPC) is a good counter against shared use security threats, albeit more expensive than normal cloud usage. In a similar manner, encrypting your data at rest is a good way to preclude an adversary reconstructing your deleted data. The combination of VPC and encrypting data at rest and in motion are usually good starting points for securing a project's data in the cloud. In addition, the PM should also ensure that a project avoids the "seven deadly sins" of user security errors as described in chapter 7.

Arranging to Use a Cloud

As recently as 2013, the pricing strategies for how much it cost to lease time, memory, computational capabilities or bandwidth within or to or from a cloud was fairly straightforward. As competition has increased between CSPs, the pricing strategies have become so complicated that the major CSPs are now providing online calculators to help the customer determine costs. Some of the factors used in these calculators include: memory used per month, bandwidth usage (where cost in may differ from cost out), types of VMs, responsiveness of the CSP to provide new VMs on demand, VPCs, and geographical limitation on where the data can be located. PMs should compare the costing options offered by different vendors, in addition to the security features provided.

Map-reduce Programming Concepts

Traditional relational (row and column) databases were very good at storing, retrieving, and analyzing structured data. As the quantity, variety, and rate of change of the data sets available in the current world have increased, they now often exceed the ability for relational databases to store and access all of this data. As a result, new methods of storing data as very long lists (RDF, Big Table, Accumulo) that can be divided among storage and processing nodes and analyzed in parallel has provided new data analysis capabilities.

The Hadoop Distributed File System (HDFS) now allows data in excess of petabytes to be stored and retrieved, while minimizing the bookkeeping burden on the user. The combination of HDFS and Hadoop map-reduce programming has made large-scale parallel processing available to the masses, and therefore applicable to many more projects than in the past. This has led to a number of discoveries of relationships not previously identified across a wide range of data sets.

In addition to being able to store and analyze structured data, another breakthrough of map-reduce programming is the ability to search and analyze *unstructured* data. Unstructured data is not in row and column format, or even in the long list formats described above. Unstructured data consists of data files in their raw form, such as web-pages, text files, binary files, and other types of files. As long as the map-reduce programmer can identify a key-value pair from this unstructured data, the map-reduce program can locate these pairs and help define a relationship between the data. While not a determination of cause-and-effect, at least identifying a previously undiscovered relationship can be valuable to a business or a researcher, and therefore useful to a PM.

Project Managers' Questions and the PMBOK® Guide

Chapters Four through Nine each present a set of questions the PM should ask regarding clouds. These chapters also describe how the five Process Groups and ten Knowledge areas from the PMBOK® Guide are applicable to the PM's project and the various types of clouds and their inherent issues. Note that as more and more organizations become regular users of clouds, many of the Questions to Ask, Process Groups and Knowledge Areas may already be addressed by an organization's standard operating procedures applied to using the cloud. Even so, it is useful to periodically ask who in your organization is currently responsible for answering some of these questions and monitoring the services provided by the CSPs.

A Final Thought

Cloud computing is here to stay, and Project Managers will become increasingly involved in using a cloud to support their projects. Hopefully this book has provided the basics for PMs to be sufficiently conversant in the basic concepts, terminologies, benefits, issues and tradeoffs of cloud computing.

Appendix A:
Knowledge Check for
Chapters 1-6

Appendices A and B are provided for the reader to review the material in this book. Students in the Cloud Computing 101 seminar frequently commented on how much the question and answer period helped them better understand the material. Since there is a lot of material to absorb, and several new mental models to remember, these questions help instill longer-term retention of the material. The material in the first six chapters is presented in Appendix A, while the material for chapters seven to nine is presented in Appendix B.

Each appendix is divided into a "questions only" section, followed by a section with both the questions and the answers.

Questions Only

1. **Name the three basic types of clouds (not the three service models for clouds).**

2. **List four reasons why it is important to be able to distinguish between different types of clouds.**

3. **Fill in the missing elements in Figure A.1:**

Cloud Type 1: Storage Cloud	☐
Cloud Type 2: Utility Cloud	☐ + ☐
Cloud Type 3: A Data-focused Cloud	☐ + ☐ + ☐

**Figure A.1 Question: The Three Types of Clouds
(Fill in the Blanks)**

4. List the three service models (sub-types) of Type 2 Computing as a Service Cloud.

5. Provide three reasons why a Storage Cloud can be useful for users.

6. Provide two reasons why a Storage Cloud is cost-effective from a provider perspective.

7. Describe a virtual machine in your own words.

8. Describe in your own words some of the benefits of a virtual machine used in clouds.

9. Describe how licensing of applications works when the software is provided by the Utility Cloud.

10. Select the best type of cloud for each type of project below.
    - If you need to run programs on a cloud, which type of cloud is preferred?
    - If you don't need to run any programs, which type of cloud is preferred?
    - If you need to manipulate huge amounts of data, which cloud is preferred?

- If you need continuity of operations support from a cloud for your organization, which type of cloud is preferred?

11. **Select the best type of cloud for each type of scenario below.**
    - You're starting a new company and want to minimize your IT infrastructure costs until your cash flow kicks in.
    - You want to coordinate activities across an international enterprise using a specialized software package.
    - You want to manage and determine trends across medical records from a nation-wide company with hundreds of terabytes of data.
    - You want to archive your company's electronic records.

12. **The following questions are related to Data-focused Clouds (Type 3 Clouds).**
    - The _____ or the _____ provide the underlying file management capability to support a Data-focused Cloud.
    - Which of these two distributed file management systems is most commonly used?
    - Describe the three elements of a traditional relational database format.
    - Describe the elements of the triple store.
    - Describe how to translate an entry from a traditional relational database to a triple store.
    - The type of program to run parallel computation in a Data-focused Cloud is called a _____ program.
    - True or False: The HDFS stores unstructured data in triple stores.
    - True or False: Accumulo runs on top of HDFS and stores data in tables in 6-tuple format.

13. **Fill in the missing arrows in Figure A.3 showing the various ways both structured and unstructured data can be processed and output in a Type 3 Cloud.**

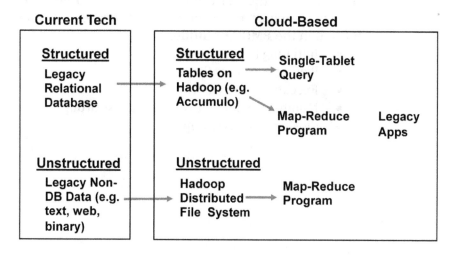

Figure A.2 Question: Structured & Unstructured Data in Type 3 Cloud (Fill in Arrows)

14. **Select either a Type 3 Data-focused Cloud or a relational database in each of the following scenarios:**
    - You want to analyze a large quantity of disparate data types from a variety of data sources with their own formats.
    - You want to analyze just under 100 terabytes of data with well-defined attributes and queries.
    - You want to analyze one petabyte of data with sparse membership in the data across a wide range of attributes.
    - A large database where new attributes of the data are being added frequently.

15. **What three columns does Accumulo have that triple stores do not?**

16. **Fill in the blank: Seeking and finding a specific data item is ____ times slower than just writing new data.**

17. **Answer True or False: Data-focused Cloud computing provides "parallel processing for the masses."**

18. Describe how the material in this book could help the Project manager perform the five process groups as defined in the PMBOK® Guide.
    - Initiating Process Group
    - Planning Process Group
    - Executing Process Group
    - Monitoring and Controlling Process Group
    - Closing Process Group

Questions with Answers

1. Name the three basic types of clouds (not the three service models for clouds)
- *Type 1 Cloud = Storage Cloud*
- *Type 2 Cloud = Utility Cloud*
- *Type 3 Cloud = Data-focused Cloud*

2. List four reasons why it is important to be able to distinguish between different types of clouds.

- *If two or more people are discussing clouds, make sure all are discussing the same types of clouds; otherwise confusion can occur and expectations might not be met.*

- *If clouds are being used on a project, know the type of cloud(s) so that you can effectively plan, execute and monitor projects that involve clouds.*

- *To assist your organization in leveraging cloud-based technologies and their various capabilities.*

- *To help your organization avoid costly mistakes by attempting to use the wrong type of cloud for an application.*

3. Fill in the missing elements in Figure A.1:

Cloud Type 1: Storage Cloud	Lots of Memory
Cloud Type 2: Utility Cloud	Lots of Memory + Virtual Machines
Cloud Type 3: A Data-focused Cloud	Lots of Memory + Hadoop Distributed File System + Hadoop map-reduce

Figure A.3: The Three Types of Clouds (With Answers)

4. List the three service models (sub-types) of Type 2 Computing as a Service Cloud.

- *Infrastructure as a Service (IaaS)*
- *Platform as a Service (PaaS)*
- *Software as a Service (SaaS)*

5. Provide three reasons why a Storage Cloud can be useful for users.

- *Protection against loss of data when a home or business computer crashes.*

- *Allows users to access these remotely stored items from wherever they can access the Internet.*

- *May be part of a continuity of operations plan to have the company records stored at a location not co-located with the main operations centers.*

6. Provide two reasons why a Storage Cloud is cost-effective from a provider perspective.

- *Cloud providers leverage economies of scale by using commodity hardware and automatic duplication to ensure secure storage inexpensively.*

- *CSPs can store fewer copies of common files with the same hash (such as a music file) as long as the copies are always available to the many users.*

7. Describe a virtual machine in your own words (any of the following answers is sufficient)

- *A software and operating system "package" that replicates all of the functionality of a personal computer but can run on almost any type of underlying hardware (Linux, Windows, or Unix).*

- *A simulated machine.*

- *A software implementation of a machine (i.e., a computer) that executes instructions (not programs) like a physical machine.*

- *A virtual machine is a piece of software that allows operating systems to be run "inside" other operating systems.*

- *A computer within a computer, implemented in software. A virtual machine emulates a complete hardware system, from processor to network card, in a self-contained, isolated software environment, enabling the simultaneous operation of otherwise incompatible operating systems.*

- *Software that allows you to take a single physical device (e.g., one PC) and run multiple instances of operating systems on it.*

8. Describe in your own words some of the benefits of a virtual machine used in clouds.

- *VMs allow the CSPs to offer their customers a wide range of operating systems and versions while running on hardware all of the same type. The economies of scale are provided by identical underlying hardware, while the VMs allow customers to select the combinations of operating system and versions that they want.*

- *VMs allow the CSPs to create and delete VMs as the customer needs change. This allows the number of VMs leased per customer to adapt quickly as customer demand changes.*

- *Each processor can sequentially run VMs of any different type.*

- *Each processor can simultaneously run multiple VMs of the same type or even of different types.*

- *The CSP only needs to patch or update the master copy of each type of VM, and create all instances of that type from the master copy. This keeps all the VMs at the most recent patch level whenever new VMs are created. It reduces maintenance costs (compared to having to patch each separate physical computer individually) and increases security (by keeping the VMs up to date).*

9. Describe how licensing of applications works when the software is provided by the Utility Cloud. *For IaaS clouds, the* customer renting the infrastructure provides the licenses. For PaaS, SaaS and DaaS clouds, the platform, software, or desktop CSPs own the licenses, and depending on the SLA, the users usually pay a fee for the use of the platform or software. The CSP owns the licenses and wraps up the cost of the software as part of their offering to the customer.

10. Select the best type of cloud for each type of project below.

- If you need to run programs on a cloud, which type of cloud is preferred? *(Answer: Type 2 Cloud if the applications are not parallel processing, while a Type 3 Cloud is preferred for parallel processing applications.)*

- If you don't need to run any programs, which type of cloud is preferred? *(Answer: A Type 1 Cloud—a Storage Cloud.)*

- If you need to manipulate huge amounts of data, which cloud is preferred? *(Answer: A Type 3 Cloud— a Data-focused Cloud.)*

- If you need continuity of operations support from a cloud for your organization, which type of cloud is preferred? *(Answer: A Type 2 Cloud to provide the replacement IT infrastructure, and possibly a Type 1 Cloud for the access to the company's archives if stored on a Type 1 Cloud. If you normally use a Data-focused Cloud in your daily operations, then a Type 3 Cloud access will also be required.)*

11. Select the best type of cloud for each type of scenario below.

- You're starting a new company and want to minimize your IT infrastructure costs until your cash flow kicks in. *(Answer: A Type 2 Cloud—a Utility Cloud to provide the initial IT infrastructure. You will also probably want this Type 2 Cloud to be an IaaS (Infrastructure as a Service) or DaaS (Desktop as a Service) service model.)*

- You want to analyze a large amount of data in ways not previously performed. *(Answer: A Type 3 Cloud—a Data-focused Cloud.)*

- You want to coordinate activities across an international enterprise using a specialized software package. *(Answer: A Type 2 Cloud with an SaaS (software as a service) service model.)*

- You want to manage and determine trends across medical records from a nation-wide company with hundreds of terabytes of data. *(Answer: A Type 3 Cloud—Data-focused Cloud.)*

- You want to archive your company's electronic records. *(Answer: A Type 1 Cloud—a Storage Cloud.)*

12. **The following questions are related to Data-focused Clouds (Type 3 Clouds).**

- The _____ or the _____ provide the underlying file management capability to support a Data-focused Cloud. *(Answer: HDFS or Sector.)*

- Which of these two distributed file management systems is most commonly used? *(Answer: HDFS—the Hadoop Distributed File System.)*

- Describe the three elements of a traditional relational database format. *(Answer: Row header, column header, and the element or entry where that row and column intersect.)*

- Describe the elements of the triple store. *(Answer: Subject, predicate, object.)*

- Describe how to translate an entry from a traditional relational database to a triple store. *(Answer: The row becomes the subject, the column becomes the predicate, and the entry becomes the object.)*

- The type of program to run parallel computation in a Data-focused Cloud is called a _____ program. *(Answer: A map-reduce program.)*

- True or False: The HDFS stores unstructured data in triple stores. *(Answer: False. The HDFS stores files in their native format, such as text, html, binary, etc.)*

- True or False: Accumulo runs on top of HDFS and stores data in tables in 6-tuple format. *(Answer: True.)*

13. Fill in the missing arrows in Figure A.3 showing the various ways both structured and unstructured data can be processed and output in a Type 3 Cloud.

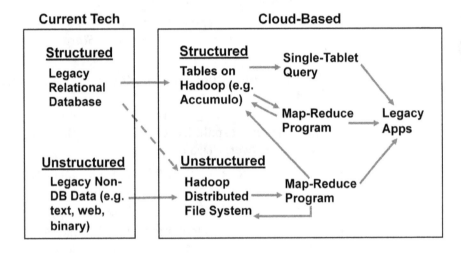

Figure A.4 Answer: Structured and Unstructured Data in Type 3 Cloud (with Arrows)

14. Select either a Type 3 Data-focused Cloud or a relational database in each of the following scenarios:

- You want to analyze a large quantity of disparate data types from a variety of data sources with their own formats. *(Answer: A Type 3 Cloud based on the variety of data types and format. This avoids the need to design a common data model as would be required in a traditional relational database.)*

- You want to analyze just under 100 terabytes of data with well-defined attributes and queries. *(Answer: A high-end traditional relational database would probably be sufficient for this scenario if one is available.)*

- You want to analyze one petabyte of data with sparse membership in the data across a wide range of attributes. *(Answer: A Type 3 Cloud. Even just storing the data in the triple store (or 5-tuple, or 6-tuple) data format will save memory compared to storing in a traditional relational database. This is before even considering the benefits of being able to parallel process the data in a Type 3 Cloud.)*

- A large database where new attributes of the data are being added frequently. *(Answer: It depends on how large the data is, but if over a few terabytes and the number of new attributes continues to be added over time, then the Type 3 Cloud would be preferred just from the perspective of how much time and effort would be required to re-define the data model and queries each time new attributes are added to the data set.)*

15. What three columns does Accumulo have that triple stores do not? *In addition to the subject (row identifier), predicate (column identifier) and object (value) that a triple store and Accumulo share, Accumulo also has a column family identifier, a security access column, and a time column.*

16. Fill in the blank: Seeking and finding a specific data item is ____ times slower than just writing new data. *(Answer: 40 times.)*

17. Answer True or False: Data-focused Cloud computing provides "parallel processing for the masses." *(Answer: True. Compared to previous specialized high-performance computing computers and programming, Big Data analysis on Data-focused Clouds is available to a much larger portion of the population.)*

18. Describe how the material in this book could help the Project manager perform the five process groups as defined in the PMBOK® Guide.

- Initiating Process Group: *Which type of cloud to use, how it will be used, what it will not be used for, CSP selection and stakeholder identification.*

- Planning Process Group: *How the cloud will be used in support of this project, how will the use of the cloud be fit into the current (or adapted) business models, how data will be encrypted in transit and at rest, what increases or decreases in risk accrue from using a cloud, and how the CSP's performance will be measured over time and by whom.*

- Executing Process Group: *If the PM's organization does not already include someone whose job will be to monitor the use of the cloud and the services provided by the CSP, then the PM will need to include someone with sufficient skills and resources to do so on the project team. In addition, during execution the PM is responsible for the communications among all stakeholders, including the project team and the CSP.*

- Monitoring and Controlling Process Group: *Monitor the CSP's performance for a third-party cloud (or monitor your cloud's performance for an in-house cloud), including the performance of map-reduce programs (if applicable), monitor and update access control parameters such as personnel transition, and monitor the CSP's meeting of the criteria in the service level agreement (SLA).*

- Closing Process Group: *Ensure access control is closed out correctly, as well as final disposition of the data stored in the cloud (either to leave it where it is or move it out).*

Appendix B: Knowledge Check for Chapters 7-9

As mentioned in Appendix A, Appendix B provides a set of questions about chapters seven to nine to help the reader retain the key points of the material. This appendix presents a set of questions about the basics of cloud security, service level agreements, and map-reduce programming. Each appendix is divided into a "questions only" section, followed by a section with both the questions and the answers.

Questions Only

1. List the three common security vulnerabilities that are common in a third-party cloud, and then describe one solution to each.

2. Describe three examples of Shared Use vulnerabilities and one of their solutions.

3. Who is responsible for each of the following security measures—the CSP, the user, or both?
   - Providing and managing user passwords.
   - Brute force DDoS attacks.
   - Checking intrusion detection system logs.
   - Installing, maintaining and monitoring firewalls to help secure the perimeter against unauthorized access.

- Installing and monitoring Intrusion Detection and Prevention Systems (IDS/IPS) to monitor activities within the cloud.
- Establishing and enforcing user password complexity policies and password change frequency.
- Maintaining up-to-date software patches on all servers and VMs.
- Using two-factor authentication for any remote access.
- Installing and managing host-based firewalls, anti-malware detection, file intrusion monitoring, log monitoring, and encryption.
- Collecting and reviewing system logs and access logs for anomalous activity.
- Physical security.
- Running anti-malware and file-integrity monitoring on the servers.
- Running regular vulnerability scans and quickly remediating any discovered vulnerabilities.
- Performing Red Team penetration testing at least annually or at the time of any significant change in the infrastructure.
- Establishing and enforcing rigorous change control processes, exercise least privilege, documented policies and procedures for password complexity and other host security capabilities.
- The firewall on the virtual private cloud.

4. **List three of the "seven deadly sins" of customer-caused cloud security failures.**

5. **What is the name of the authorization process for vendors providing clouds for unclassified and sensitive but unclassified (SBU) data?**

6. **List three of the questions you might want to ask your CSP with respect to security.**

7. **List three of the questions you might want to ask with respect to your project team and home organization**

about using the cloud? (For example, who is responsible for what?)

8. **Name the four types of cloud deployment models.**

9. **Address the following scenarios:**
   - How do you ensure that the hand-off from one cloud service provider to another is complete?
   - What is one of the best ways to select among competing CSPs?
   - How do you evaluate the value of a CSP's guarantees?
   - What is one way of transferring risk of loss of data availability?

10. **Questions on Cloud deployment models:**
    - True/False: A private cloud is one that you set up yourself.
    - True/False: A hybrid cloud is a combination of private, community, and/or public clouds.
    - Describe a community cloud.
    - Who owns and manages a public cloud?

11. Fill in the headers for the Figure that shows how the cloud types, service models, deployment models and owners fit together.

		Hybrid			In-House	3rd Party
		Private	Community	Public		
Cloud Type 1: Storage Cloud						
Cloud Type 2: Utility Cloud	IaaS : XaaS Variants					
	PaaS : XaaS Variants					
	SaaS : XaaS Variants					
Cloud Type 3: Data-focused Cloud						

Figure B.1 Question: Fill in the Blanks in this Figure

12. Describe three variables often used in cloud pricing strategies.

13. True/False: The charge for transferring data is always the same whether the data is entering or leaving the cloud.

14. True/False: Many CSPs use an online calculator to help potential users price cloud usage.

15. True/False Exercises for Designing Programs in a Cloud:
   - True/False: A map-reduce program is a database query.
   - True/False: In a map-reduce program, I need to tell the cloud where every data item is located in order to access it.

- True/False: Map-reduce programs can only be written in Java.
- True/False: I can write a map-reduce program to retrieve selected subsets of data in addition to total counts.

16. **True/False: An RDF format (triple store) facilitates parallel processing.**

17. **True/False: A query in Accumulo runs in parallel against multiple Accumulo tablets in the cloud.**

18. **True/False: A map-reduce program run against unstructured data must identify a key-value pair in order to return any useful data.**

19. **Describe the two basic ways to address "dirty" data.**

Questions with Answers

1. List the three common security vulnerabilities that are common in a third-party cloud, and then describe one solution to each.

- *Physical security and geographical issues*
    - i. *Solution to Physical: CSPs enforce strict access control to its physical spaces.*
    - ii. *Solution to Geographical: Selecting regional restrictions on where your data may be stored.*

- *Communications security*
    - i. *Solution: Encrypt communications to and from the cloud.*
    - ii. *Solution: Two-factor authentication for remote access.*

- *Shared use*
    - i. *Solutions: See answers to next question.*

2. Describe three examples of Shared Use vulnerabilities and one of their solutions.

- *Co-residency and side-channel attacks*
    - i. *Solution: Limited cloud access, such as a virtual private cloud (VPC) or building your own private cloud.*
    - ii. *Solution: Encrypting data at rest and "Home Alone" type software.*

- *Recoverable data deletion*
    - i. *Solution: Encrypting data at rest.*

- *Distributed Denial of Service attacks*
    - i. *Answer: Against ransom-type denial of service attacks, ensure good communications security practice, multi-factor authentication, strict access control, and training to prevent successful social engineering attacks.*
    - ii. *Answer: Against brute force DDOS attacks, the CSP is responsible for maintaining connectivity and availability.*

3. Who is responsible for each of the following security measures—the CSP, the user, or both?

- Providing and managing user passwords. *(Answer: User)*

- Brute force DDoS attacks. (Answer: CSP)

- Checking intrusion detection system logs. *(Answer: Both CSP and User)*

- Installing, maintaining and monitoring firewalls to help secure the perimeter against unauthorized access. *(Answer: CSP)*

- Installing and monitoring Intrusion Detection and Prevention Systems (IDS/IPS) to monitor activities within the cloud. *(Answer: CSP)*

- Establishing and enforcing user password complexity policies and password change frequency. *(Answer: User)*

- Maintaining up-to-date software patches on all servers and VMs. *(Answer: CSP)*

- Using two-factor authentication for any remote access. *(Answer: Both CSP and User)*

- Installing and managing host-based firewalls, anti-malware detection, file intrusion monitoring, log monitoring, and encryption. *(Answer: User)*

- Collecting and reviewing system logs and access logs for anomalous activity. *(Answer: Both CSP and User)*

- Physical security. *(Answer: CSP)*

- Running anti-malware and file-integrity monitoring on the servers. *(Answer: CSP)*

- Running regular vulnerability scans and quickly remediating any discovered vulnerabilities. *(Answer: Both CSP and User)*

- Performing Red Team penetration testing at least annually or at the time of any significant change in the infrastructure. *(Answer: Both CSP and User)*

- Establishing and enforcing rigorous change control processes, exercise least privilege, documented policies and procedures for password complexity and other host security capabilities. *(Answer: CSP)*

- The firewall on the virtual private cloud. *(Answer: Either the CSP or the User. If the CSP does not provide one, the user must provide one.)*

4. List three of the "seven deadly sins" of customer-caused cloud security failures. *Any three of the following answers are sufficient:*

- *Failure to administer the firewall at the perimeter of a virtual environment.*

- *Failure to monitor perimeter firewall for inbound and outbound attacks.*

- *Failure to establish and enforce good password policies.*

- *Failure to install operating system and application patches in a timely fashion.*

- *Failure to install, run, and patch anti-malware software and host-based firewalls*

- *Failure to actively monitor host-based security controls for sign of compromise.*

- *Failure to educate users on the importance of following good security practices.*

5. What is the name of the authorization process for vendors providing clouds for unclassified and sensitive but unclassified (SBU) data? *(Answer: FedRAMP.)*

6. List three of the questions you might want to ask your CSP with respect to security. *Any three of the following answers are sufficient:*

- *When my data is loaded into the cloud, where will it be physically located (by broad geographical location)?*

- *Does the CSP provide options for where my data will be physically located?*

- *When data is replicated, what constraints are applied to where the data is physically copied to?*

- *How is physical security provided at the CSP?*

- *Who gets access to the physical location, and how is that monitored?*

- *How does the CSP plan to protect against brute force DDoS attacks if they occur?*

7. List three of the questions you might want to ask with respect to your project team and home organization about using the cloud? (For example, who is responsible for what?) *Any three of the following answers are sufficient:*

- *Do I want to use a third-party vendor cloud or a home-built cloud?*

- *How are communications to be secured to and from the cloud?*

- *How will data at rest be encrypted?*

- *Who will monitor that the secure communications to and from the cloud are and remain secure?*

- *Who will configure and monitor the organization's firewall logs to ensure best security practices?*

- *Who will install and upgrade anti-malware software logs when the user applies them in a cloud?*

- *Who will monitor the intrusion detection systems and firewall logs to determine whether intrusions are being attempted or have occurred?*

- *Who will install and monitor the patch upgrades for operating systems and applications used by the project in the cloud?*

- *Who sets and enforces user password policies?*

- *Who educates project team members in good cyber security practices?*

- *Who will perform vulnerability scans and penetration testing, and how often?*

8. Name the four types of cloud deployment models:
- *Private*
- *Community*
- *Public*
- *Hybrid*

9. Address the following scenarios:
- How do you ensure that the hand-off from one cloud service provider to another is complete? *(Answer: Have the data from the first CSP returned to you before you send the data to the new CSP. This transfer can be done in stages if your local memory is limited.)*
- What is one of the best ways to select among competing CSPs? *(Answer: Compare the performance of two or more CSPs using sample data and usage. This may be set up entirely by the user without a formal competition among vendors.)*
- How do you evaluate the value of a CSP's guarantees? *(Answer: Perform a risk assessment and determine the cost of data loss, data breach, or lack of availability. Then compare the compensation provided by the CSP and determine whether that compensation is sufficient to cover the risk.)*
- What is one way of transferring risk of loss of data availability? *(Answer: Insurance from the CSP or from an independent underwriter.)*

10. Questions on cloud deployment models:
- True/False: A private cloud is one that you set up yourself. *(Answer: False. A private cloud is one that limits the access to the cloud to one user organization. A cloud you set up yourself may be a private cloud, but many CSPs provide private clouds and VPCs.)*
- True/False: A hybrid cloud is a combination of private, community, and/or public clouds. *(Answer: True.)*
- Describe a community cloud. *(Answer: A community cloud is one where more than one organization is*

allowed access to the cloud, but the cloud is not open to the general public. Access is limited to membership in the community.)

- Who owns and manages a public cloud? *(Answer: A cloud service provider or CSP.)*

11. Fill in the headers for the Figure that shows how the cloud types, service models, deployment models and owners fit together.

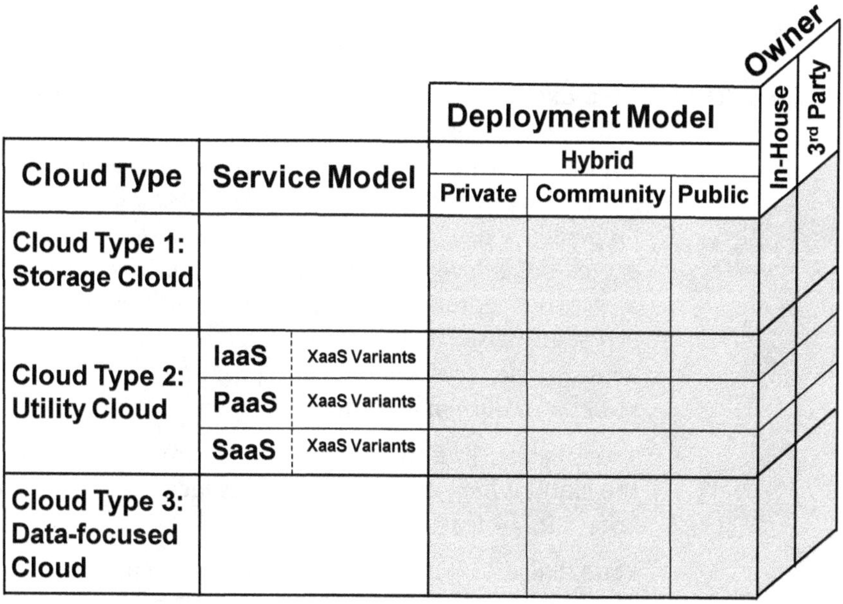
Owner
In-House
3rd Party
Deployment Model
Hybrid
Private
Community
Public
Cloud Type
Service Model
Cloud Type 1: Storage Cloud
Cloud Type 2: Utility Cloud
IaaS
XaaS Variants
PaaS
XaaS Variants
SaaS
XaaS Variants
Cloud Type 3: Data-focused Cloud

Figure B.2 Answer: Relate Cloud Types, Service Models, Deployment Models and Owners

12. Describe three variables often used in cloud pricing strategies. *Any three of the following factors is sufficient:*

- *Memory used per hour or per month*
- *Number and variety of VMs used*
- *Bandwidth used to get data into or out of the cloud*
- *Speed of responsiveness to newly requested VMs (faster response costs more)*

- *User location limits to geographical distribution of the cloud*

- *The security features included in the CSP's offering*

13. True/False: The charge for transferring data is always the same whether the data is entering or leaving the cloud. *(Answer: False. Some CSPs charge more for sending data out of the cloud than into the cloud.)*

14. True/False: Many CSPs use an online calculator to help potential users price cloud usage. *(Answer: True.)*

15. True/False Exercises for Designing Programs in a Cloud:
- True/False: A map-reduce program is a database query. *(Answer: False. A map-reduce program is more powerful than a legacy database query, but a map-reduce program can be sufficiently simple so as to act as a traditional database query on a distributed structured database. In addition, a map-reduce program can also be run against unstructured data, while a legacy query can only be run against structured data in a database.)*

- True/False: In a map-reduce program, I need to tell the cloud where every data item is located in order to access it. *(Answer: False.)*

- True/False: Map-reduce programs can only be written in Java. *(Answer: False. They can also be written in Python, LISP, and other languages.)*

- True/False: I can write a map-reduce program to retrieve selected subsets of data in addition to total counts. *(Answer: True.)*

16. True/False: An RDF format (triple store) facilitates parallel processing. *(Answer: True.)*

17. True/False: A query in Accumulo runs in parallel against multiple Accumulo tablets in the cloud. *(Answer: False. Queries run sequentially. Map-reduce programs run in parallel against Accumulo tablets.)*

18.   True/False: A map-reduce program run against unstructured data must identify a key-value pair in order to return any useful data. *(Answer: True.)*

19. Describe the two basic ways to address "dirty" data.

- *The first is to do "data cleansing" to detect and remove or fix data errors before running map-reduce programs against the data. (Map-reduce programs can also be used specifically to detect and remove data errors as part of the data cleansing process.)*

- *The second is to write every map-reduce program with its own error detection and mitigation code embedded in the program.*

References

Alert Logic Cloud Security Report, Spring 2014 -
https://www.alertlogic.com/resources/cloud-security-report/

Amazon EC2 Instances - http://aws.amazon.com/ec2/instance-types/

Amazon Web Services (AWS) Elastic Compute Cloud (EC2) -
http://aws.amazon.com/ec2/

Amazon Web Services (AWS) Elastic Compute Cloud (EC2) Pricing -
http://aws.amazon.com/ec2/pricing/

Amazon Web Services (AWS) GovCloud (US) Region - Government Cloud
Computing - http://aws.amazon.com/govcloud-us/

Apache Hadoop Encryption - Nov. 2014;
http://hadoop.apache.org/docs/current/hadoop-project-dist/hadoop-
hdfs/TransparentEncryption.html

Apache Hadoop Map-reduce Tutorial -
https://hadoop.apache.org/docs/r1.2.1/mapred_tutorial.html

AWS GovCloud (US) Region - Government Cloud Computing -
http://aws.amazon.com/govcloud-us/

Babcock, Charles, "CloudBees Drops PaaS, Shifts To Continuous
Integration," 22 Sept 2014 -
http://www.informationweek.com/cloud/software-as-a-service/cloudbees-
drops-paas-shifts-to-continuous-integration/d/d-id/1315935

Badger, Lee, et al., *US Government Cloud Computing Technology Roadmap
Vol. I, Release 1.0 (Draft): High-Priority Requirements to Further USG Agency
Cloud Computing Adoption,* NIST Special Publication 500-293, 2011 -
http://www.nist.gov/itl/cloud/upload/SP_500_293_volumeI-2.pdf

Badger, Lee, et al., *US Government Cloud Computing Technology Roadmap
Vol. II Release 1.0 (Draft): Useful Information for Cloud Adopters,* NIST

Special Publication 500-293, 2011 -
http://www.nist.gov/itl/cloud/upload/SP_500_293_volumeII.pdf

Baxley, Barry, Dell Cloud Services Security Consultant, 2014, Private Correspondence

Beal, Vangie, "Structured Data," Webopedia, 20 August 2014 -
http://www.webopedia.com/TERM/S/structured_data.html

Bigelow, Stephen, "Do we still need cloud data encryption?" Tech Target, Dec 2014 -
http://searchcloudcomputing.techtarget.com/answer/Do-we-still-need-cloud-data-encryption

Boisvert, Michelle, "Cloud computing adoption numbers don't add up to vendor noise," *Tech Target,* April 2013 -
http://searchcloudcomputing.techtarget.com/feature/Cloud-computing-adoption-numbers-dont-add-up-to-vendor-noise/

Burt, Jeffrey, "Amazon Reboots Cloud Servers to Patch Xen Hypervisor," eweek.com, 27 Sept 2014 -
http://www.eweek.com/cloud/amazon-reboots-cloud-servers-to-patch-xen-hypervisor.html

CloudBees - http://www.cloudbees.com/

Cloudera.com Map-reduce Tutorial -
http://www.cloudera.com/content/cloudera-content/cloudera-docs/HadoopTutorial/CDH4/Hadoop-Tutorial.html

Cloud Security Alliance - https://cloudsecurityalliance.org/

Cohen, Reuven, "New Cloud Computing Insurance Attempts to Solve Cloud Liability Concerns for Service Providers," *Forbes online*, 24 April 2013 -
http://www.forbes.com/sites/reuvencohen/2013/04/24/new-cloud-computing-insurance-trys-to-solve-cloud-liability-concerns-for-service-providers/

Dark Reading, "Researchers Develop Cross-VM Side-Channel Attack," 1 Nov 2012 -
http://www.darkreading.com/cloud-security/167901092/security/attacks-breaches/240012743/researchers-develop-cross-vm-side-channel-attack.html

Dot Cloud - http://www.dotcloud.com/

Duhigg, Charles, "How Companies Learn Your Secrets," *New York Times,* 16 February 2012 -
http://www.nytimes.com/2012/02/19/magazine/shopping-habits.html

Engineyard - http://www.engineyard.com/

Facebook, "How Does Facebook Suggest Tags?" -
https://www.facebook.com/help/122175507864081

FedRAMP Compliant Cloud Systems, GSA 2014 -
http://cloud.cio.gov/fedramp/cloud-systems

FedRAMP, Concept of Operations (CONOPs), version 1.2, 27 July 2012 -
http://cloud.cio.gov/sites/default/files/documents/files/CONOPS_V1.2_
072712_0.pdf

FedRAMP portal - http://cloud.cio.gov/fedramp

Gibson, Dan, "Map-reduce: How to," University of Wisconsin Madison, 31 July 2010 - http://pages.cs.wisc.edu/~gibson/mapReduceTutorial.html

Goldberg, "Survey of Virtual Machine Research," 2002 -
http://infolab.stanford.edu/~manku/quals/summaries/wong-vmsurvey.htm

Google App Engine - http://code.google.com/appengine/

Google Apps for Work -
http://www.google.com/apps/intl/en/business/index.html

Google Compute Engine (GCE) - https://cloud.google.com/compute/

Gourley, Bob, "Georgia Institute of Technology Wins for Innovative Crowdsourcing Disaster Relief System," June 18, 2014 -
http://entrepreneurs.ulitzer.com/node/3108558

Gregg, Michael, "10 Security Concerns for Cloud Computing,"
GlobalKnowledge.com, 2010 -
http://viewer.media.bitpipe.com/1078177630_947/1268847180_5/WP_VI_10
SecurityConcernsCloudComputing.pdf

Greenberg, Adam, "Code Spaces shuts down following DDoS extortion, deletion of sensitive data," *SC Magazine*, 19 June 2014 -
http://www.scmagazine.com/code-spaces-shuts-down-following-ddos-extortion-deletion-of-sensitive-data/article/356774/

Heroku.com - http://www.heroku.com/

Higginbotham, Stacey, "Why Verizon Bought Terremark for $1.4B," GIGAOM Research, 27 January 2011 - http://gigaom.com/2011/01/27/why-verizon-bought-terremark-for-1-4b

Hoff, Todd, "Numbers Everyone Should Know," 18 February 2009 - http://highscalability.com/numbers-everyone-should-know

Holtsnider, Bill and Brian D. Jaffe, *IT Manager's Handbook: Getting Your New Job Done, 2nd Ed.,* Morgan Kauffman Publishers, October 2006 - http://www.itmanagershandbook.com/glossary.html

IBM Case Studies, "Explore Customer Stories" - http://www-03.ibm.com/software/businesscasestudies/us/en/corp

IBM Cloud Computing - http://www.ibm.com/cloud-computing/us/en/iaas.html

IBM Connections Cloud S2 - http://www-03.ibm.com/software/products/en/ibm-smartcloud-engage

IBM, "Meteolytix generates precise sales forecasts for bakery branches," 2011 - http://public.dhe.ibm.com/common/ssi/ecm/en/ytc03358deen/ YTC03358DEEN.PDF

IBM, "Softlayer Fuels Hybrid Cloud Growth for IBM with New Clients and Services," Armonk, NY, 14 July 2014 - http://www.ibm.com/news/ca/en/2014/07/14/r150337t68074f95.html

IBM Watson, "IBM Watson platform enables more effective healthcare preapproval decisions using evidence-based learning," June 2014 - http://www.ibm.com/smarterplanet/us/en/ibmwatson/assets/pdfs/ WellPoint_Case_Study_IMC14792.pdf

Interglot, "Virtual Machine" Interglot Translation Dictionary - http://www.interglot.com/dictionary/en/en/translate/virtual%20machine

Kissel, Richard, Matthew Scholl, Steven Skolochenko, Xing Li, "Guidelines for Media Sanitation, NIST Special Publication 800-88; September 2006 - http://csrc.nist.gov/publications/nistpubs/800-88/NISTSP800-88_with-errata.pdf

Krzyzanowski, Paul "Distributed Systems, Map-reduce," 2011 - https://www.cs.rutgers.edu/~pxk/417/notes/content/mapreduce.html

Law, Emily, "Image Processing on the Cloud," NASA LMMP, 14 July 2012 - http://trs-new.jpl.nasa.gov/dspace/bitstream/2014/42723/1/12-0331_A1b.pdf

Lin, Jimmy and Chris Dyer, "Data-Intensive Text Processing with Map-reduce," 31 May 2009 - http://www.slideshare.net/inboklee/map-reduce-tutorialslides

Liu, Fang, et al., *NIST Cloud Computing Reference Architecture*, Special Publication 500-292, September 2011 - http://www.nist.gov/customcf/get_pdf.cfm?pub_id=909505

Lowry, Bill, Director Cloud Services at Radware, "Five Burning Security Issues in Cloud Computing," IT Business Edge, 2014 - http://www.itbusinessedge.com/slideshows/five-burning-security-issues-in-cloud-computing.html

Lunar Mapping and Modeling Portal (LMMP) - http://www.lmmp.nasa.gov

Lyman, Peter, and Hal R. Varian, "How Much Information?" 18 October 2000 - http://www2.sims.berkeley.edu/research/projects/how-much-info/how-much-info.pdf%20-%20page=110

Mell, Peter, and Timothy Grance, *The NIST Definition of Cloud Computing*, National Institute of Standards and Technology, NIST Special Publication 800-145, 2011 - http://csrc.nist.gov/publications/nistpubs/800-145/SP800-145.pdf

Mennig, Don, "2014 Cloud of Dreams Infographic," *Cloud IQ*, 15 September 2014 - http://blog.evolveip.net/index.php/2014/09/15/2014-cloud-of-dreams-infographic/

Microsoft Azure - http://azure.microsoft.com

Microsoft Office Online - http://office.microsoft.com/en-us/web-apps/

Mills, Mark, "The Cloud Begins with Coal: Big Data, Big Networks, Big Infrastructure, and Big Power," National Mining Association, American Coalition for Clean Coal Energy, August 2013 - http://www.tech-pundit.com/wp-content/uploads/2013/07/Cloud_Begins_With_Coal.pdf

Nikiforakis, Nick and Günes Acar, "Browser Fingerprinting and the Online-Tracking Arms Race," *IEEE Spectrum*, 25 July 2014 - http://spectrum.ieee.org/computing/software/browser-fingerprinting-and-the-onlinetracking-arms-race

NIST Big Data Public Working Group (NBD-PWG), Draft NIST Big Data Interoperability Framework: Volume 1, Definitions, Version 1; 2014 - http://bigdatawg.nist.gov/_uploadfiles/BD_Vol1-Definitions_V1Draft_Pre-release.pdf

NIST, *Draft NIST Cloud Computing Security Reference Architecture*, Special Publication 500-299, undated - http://collaborate.nist.gov/twiki-cloud-computing/pub/CloudComputing/CloudSecurity/NIST_Security_Reference_Architecture_2013.05.15_v1.0.pdf

Noll, Michael G., "Writing an Hadoop MapReduce Program in Python," 2011 - http://www.michael-noll.com/tutorials/writing-an-hadoop-mapreduce-program-in-python/

Open Cloud Consortium (OCC), "Sector," 2013 - http://opencloudconsortium.org/

Gregory Piatetsky, "Did Target Really Predict a Teen's Pregnancy? The Inside Story," *KD Nuggets*, May 7, 2014 - http://www.kdnuggets.com/ 2014/05/ target-predict-teen-pregnancy-inside-story.html

Pivotal Initiative - http://www.pivotal.io/

PMBOK® Guide - http://www.pmi.org/pmbok-guide-and-standards/pmbok-guide.aspx

Rackspace Managed Cloud - http://www.rackspace.com/cloud/

Research at Google, "Map-reduce: The Programming Model and Practice," Tutorial, 2009 - http://research.google.com/pubs/pub36249.html

Ristenpart, Thomas, Eran Tromer, Hovav Shacham, Stefan Savage, "Hey You, Get Off of My Cloud: Exploring Information Leakage on Third-Party Compute Clouds," University of California San Diego, *CCS'09*, November 9—13, 2009 - http://cseweb.ucsd.edu/~hovav/dist/cloudsec.pdf

Sahara Project, OpenStack, 2014 - https://wiki.openstack.org/wiki/Sahara

Salesforce - http://www.salesforce.com/

Salesforce Products Overview - http://www.salesforce.com/products/

Schultz, Michael and Raj Jain, "A Survey of Cloud Security Issues and Offerings," a Project Report, Washington University in St. Louis; 2011 - http://www.cse.wustl.edu/~jain/cse571-11/ftp/cloud/index.html# ristenpart09; http://www.cse.wustl.edu/~jain/cse571-11/ftp/cloud.pdf

SearchCloudComputing, "Thirteen cloud service providers to watch in 2013," *Search Cloud Computing*, 28 February 2013 - http://searchcloudcomputing.techtarget.com/photostory/2240178752/ Thirteen-cloud-service-providers-to-watch-in-2013/1/PaaS-IaaS-providers-keep-the-cloud-market-moving

Sun, Yunchan, Junsheng Zhang, Yongpin Xiong, and Guangyu Zhu, "Data Security and Privacy in Cloud Computing," *International Journal of Distributed Sensor Networks,* Volume 2014 (2014), Article ID 190903 - http://www.hindawi.com/search/all/190903/

Thought Works (Heroku) - http://success.heroku.com/thoughtworks-flood

Ubuntu, "Virtual Machine" - https://help.ubuntu.com/community/Glossary#V

White, Tim, *Hadoop: The Definitive Guide, Third Edition*, O'Reilly, Cambridge, 2012

Wikipedia, "Apache Accumulo," 2014 - http://en.wikipedia.org/wiki/Apache_Accumulo

Wikipedia, "Apache_Hadoop," 2013 - http://en.wikipedia.org/wiki/Apache_Hadoop

Wikipedia, "Big Data," 2014 - http://en.wikipedia.org/wiki/Big_data

Wikipedia, "NaviSite," 2015 - http://en.wikipedia.org/wiki/NaviSite

Wikipedia, "Petabyte," 2014 - http://en.wikipedia.org/wiki/Petabyte

Wikipedia, "Resource Description Framework," 2014 - http://en.wikipedia.org/wiki/Resource_Description_Framework

Wikipedia, Side-channel Attack, 2014 - http://itlaw.wikia.com/wiki/Side_channel_attack

Wikipedia, "Unstructured Data," 2014 - http://en.wikipedia.org/wiki/Unstructured_data

Wikipedia, "Virtual Machine" - http://en.wikipedia.org/wiki/Virtual_machine

Williams, Alex, "Hosting Provider Savvis Is Now CenturyLink Technology Solutions," *Tech Crunch*, 21 January 2014 - http://techcrunch.com/2014/01/21/hosting-provider-savvis-is-now-centurylink-technology-solutions/

Yahoo Developer Hadoop Tutorial - https://hadoop.apache.org/docs/r1.2.1/mapred_tutorial.html

Zhang, Yinqian, An Juels, Alina Oprea, and Michael Reiter, "HomeAlone: Co-Residency Detection in the Cloud via Side-Channel Analysis," IEEE Symposium on Security and Privacy 2011 - http://www.emc.com/emc-plus/rsa-labs/staff/bios/ajuels/publications/HomeAlone.pdf

About the Author

Dr. Patrick D. Allen, PMP, is a senior researcher and practitioner at the Johns Hopkins University Applied Physics Laboratory in Laurel, Maryland. During his 30 years of project management experience, he has assisted a wide range of clients understand and employ new technologies to accomplish their goals. By translating new technologies into more comprehensible mental models, Allen guides newcomers to a new field using simple and familiar concepts.

Dr. Allen has been a certified Project Management Professional for 10 years, during which time he has presented a successful seminar series on cloud computing and project management. He is a retired Colonel in the US Army Reserves, a former Director of the Military Operations Research Society, and a former Adjunct Professor for Old Dominion University teaching software project management, systems analysis and systems engineering.

Dr. Allen has a B.S. in Physics, an M.S. and PhD in Operations Research, and a second masters in Strategic Studies. An international consultant for the United Kingdom, Canada and Sweden, he is the author of *Information Operations Planning* (Artech House), as well as three book chapters, and numerous papers and articles.

He welcomes comments and feedback:

Dr. Patrick D. Allen, PMP
Johns Hopkins University Applied Physics Laboratory
11100 Johns Hopkins Road
Laurel, MD 20723-6099

Patrick.Allen@PatrickAllenPubs.com
http://www.PatrickAllenPubs.com